Missing Providence
A Frequency Anthology

Frequency Writers

Edited by Ben Williams

Copyright © 2015 Frequency Writers

All rights reserved.

ISBN: 1516871154
ISBN-13: 978-1516871155

ACKNOWLEDGMENTS

Thanks also to friends from the Frequency community who made this project possible: Amy Pickworth, Everett Epstein, Heather Jackson, Heather Price, Hollis Mickey, Janaya Kizzie, Jenna Legault, Kate Wells, Louise Moulton, Nina Pratt, Renee Soto, Rosalynde Vas Dias, Steve & Dawn Porter of ARIA, Susan Tacent, & Victor Wildman.

Our thanks to the City of Providence's Department of Arts, Culture + Tourism, in particular Director Lynne McCormack, Deputy Director Stephanie P. Fortunato & Marketing Coordinator Michael Christofaro, for help funding this project.

And for opening their spaces to the writers in our community, thanks to Ada Books & the Providence Public Library.

ABOUT FREQUENCY

Frequency is a growing community of writers based in Providence, Rhode Island. Through workshops, free events, talks, readings, and open mics, we aim to engage writers of all levels of experience, ages, and backgrounds. Our offerings are designed both to challenge and support writers, while also encouraging collaboration with other local creative communities. Frequency is a moving creation of the people in it.

Visit us at frequencywriters.org!

CONTENTS

Part I: Panorama

Saving Providence: Shirley Utterback	3
The Talk About Scarlet: A.M. Anderson	4
No Glass to Hold These Hours: Mary Ann Mayer	5
Manna: Juli Anna J. Herndon	6
Falling into Darkness: Alyssa Copeland	7
Such a Lovely Light: Kik Williams	8
Providence: Diana DeCesaris Champa	9
A Box of Skyscrapers: Abigail Clarkin	10
People Don't Know: Wayne Renkin	11
Impressions: Providence: Erin Perfect	12
Purchased by Love: Mary Ann Mayer	13
Collected Poems: Wendy Grossman	15
Lighteater: Nicholas Morley	17
Silent Meeting: 2015: Adele Bourne	22
Aftermath, 2013: Sienna Zeilinger	23
We Are Providence: Nada Samih Rotondo	24

Part II: Encounters

Christian Hill: Janaya Kizzie	29
"Bella Apocalypse,": Adele Bourne	30
Passage / The Museum: J-Coby Wayne	31
On Empire Street: Mary Ann Mayer	33
Always be the same amount: Alexander Smith	34
Old Mills & Cheap Rent: Dan Shewan	35
Ascending Without Orpheus: Ira Schaeffer	39
Quiet: Kylie Wyman	40
A woman crossing Thayer St / Before dinner, I stop at Coffee Exchange: A.M. Anderson	41
britomart, burgundy bicycle: Juli Anna J. Herndon	42
Planted for Spring: C.A. Demi	43
Roger Williams Park: Michael Crowley	45
Playing Hide & Seek in the Garden of Heroes: Julie Danho	47
Collected Poems: Nancy Jasper	48
TRI-X Providence: Susan Tacent	50
In a Blizzard: James Crews	56

Part III: Departure
Collected Poems: Aaron Samuels	59
Sens Francois: Alyssa Copeland	61
The Expiration Date: Avelino de Castro	63
Collected Poems: Robin Dionne	66
Providence: Antonia Farzan	68
Wynton Marsalis at the VMA: David O'Connell	70
In Response to Sam Teitel's Letter to NY: Astrid Drew	71
Funeral: Kik Williams	73
Necromancer: Meghan Friedmann	74
False Starts (Kelsey): Everett Epstein	75
Olneyville Graffiti Update: Jacob Khepler	78
Taking the Plunge: Heather Jackson	81
The Order: Karen Haskell	84
From the Armory District to the Suburbs: Liz Kenyon	89
Dear Urban Chicken Farmer of Providence: Amanda Faith Poirier	92
Acknowledgements: Thomas Brendler	94
Mourning Glory: Adele Bourne	96
Peculiar Reflection: Jennifer Geller	97
We Move the Machines: Claire Robinson	99

INTRODUCTION

From its inception, this project sought to "map" out the city, to manifest the city through the written work of its residents. The cartographic approach failed—pieces of the city weren't represented or certain texts weren't firmly rooted in specific places. This failure reminds us of any anthology's limitations. Ultimately, these collected texts offer an array of perspectives, marking a particular moment in time while also providing a permanent testament to the city. We hope that they serve as the beginning of a conversation about the writer's experience in Providence.

The construction of this anthology involved a great deal of outreach to organizations and individuals in the community. As a result, we included writers within and outside of Frequency's circles.

Part I gives us a "Panorama" of the city, views from above or afar, temporally and spatially. In Part II, we experience multiple "Encounters" within Providence—of self, of others, or of the city as a character. Finally, Part III functions as a point of "Departure," an opportunity to look backwards and move forwards.

In a practice often predicated on solitude, Frequency endeavors to bring writers together to inspire their creative impulses. We encourage readers to view the anthology as a continual collective process. Therefore, we have included blank pages at the end of this book to make space for the voices missing from this rendition of the text. As our voices recede, we wish for yours to increase.

Ben Williams, Editor
September 2015

Industrial Trust Company under construction [2]

PART I

PANORAMA

Frequency Writers

Saving Providence
Shirley Utterback

Old red brick flakes quietly into history.
Tired mills, retired tasks, forgotten
factories, so full of hope for future fortunes,
become silent, empty shells, arson bait
or glorified gentrification.
Prairie Avenue art galleries feature perilous
graffiti echoing boarding house artistry
unlisted in RISD's museum guidebook.

Pedimented doorways, Palladian windows,
rescued from despair, announce a preservation feat
not open to past immigrants scrambling
to find a place of safe content.

Multi-cultural waves flowed over bricked streets,
where shutters waited to protect each house's
thick, wavy glass eyes, distorting scenes within,
where lace makers crowded in with laborers,
seamen with coopers, planters with seamstresses.

Cornices embellished old English house designs,
careful clapboards embracing each story
held within, each story told over and over
as families moved in and out,
pushed by wealth or want.
Providence—guardian, caretaker—
still needed to watch over its dependents.

The Talk About Scarlet
A.M. Anderson

Talk about
any New England town consists
of people on their way to things
that they should be doing,
things others are doing,
those things which
two are doing too
much and one
who
remembers where
a landmark once stood;
where something
else now stands
in place.

Interstate 195 under construction [3]

No Glass To Hold These Hours
Mary Ann Mayer

That song,
it changes people.
    Finds you inside your life
      on your way to doing other things.
That song is time.

Beautiful, how the air grows around it,
stretching, expectant, full as can be
      the song quivers the air
      quickens the need
      it weaves and attaches
like arousal rouses by degree.

Iridescent chords are an enchanting thing.
In the small city midnight…at Nick-a-Nees
there's gladness inside this place.
      The street shakes out its hardness and ease,
numbered and blessed.

I like the half-tone light, the settling-in sounds.
Dominoes, applause, side-talk,
    a certain smolder and hush….
And the satin-eyed bartender pours.

There is no glass to hold these hours!

Jubilant, it overflows! Music, muse,
the troubadour's voice, torch
    beneath the treble, his gaze
    obsidian (over the room), light on faces,
a warmth. And how we dance!

Eyes open, eyes shut doesn't matter,
hands clasped for hours, bodies
    obliging song obliging bodies
to the tipping point, brim,
leaning on the song,
    as if it is holding us up…
loving the song

    as if, as if
it were not destined to leave.

MANNA
Juli Anna J Herndon

mechanical starlings,
royal pillars & a bat box.

punctured mattress -
let the mouse go.

apricot
a riot of sparrows

sodden wonderbread,
algae on velour -

for rent, for sale
batting? dryer lint? fuzzy fungus?

pine-urine scent of juniper
enormous rhododendron
                    trust us

pastures – puddles

think they'll get along without me?

tulipped grotto
a spire, a spout!

found: a fingernail -
oh, mother mystic.

sunflowers
bowed and blackened

3 more mattresses
unfathomed bend

glasshouse penitentiary
staircase of sun.

Falling into Darkness
Alyssa Copeland

In the darkness of my room,
at the tender age of twelve,
I practiced my cursing.
Earlier, on the bus home,
my first time to public school alone
after a childhood spent with Christ,
I had muttered them under my breath
and giggled with each bad word
that I dared to say aloud -
while those same words were screamed
over my head and reverberated off the metal seats
by the other children on the bus.

But then, with only my nightlight to witness,
it was me and God.
The solemnity of that moment
quieted my sinful tongue.
But the words still flowed through my mind,
weighing me down with guilt
because good girls don't swear;
      they wear dresses and black shiny shoes,
      read their Bibles and pray every night,
      turn the other cheek when slapped,
      stay silent in the face of tribulation.

No one was a good girl
like the ones at my old Baptist school,
who wore their Sunday dresses every day
so the teachers could praise their piety to God
but didn't realize their black shoes were scuffed
after kicking me under the desks and behind the jungle gym.
They could quote passages from the Bible
about showing love and mercy to mankind
while they prayed to each other in journals
and little letters in my desk
that I never woke up tomorrow.
Good girls are the ones who laughed
when I finally began to cry from the pain,
two swollen cheeks turned.

No matter what I did,
goodness and mercy would not come to me
like it did for them.
So I closed my eyes to practice again,
cursing defiantly in the silence,
as I imagined each of their perfect Godly faces.

Such a Lovely Light
Kik Williams

Edna your sonnet #42   how the hell did you forget all those
arms that lain under your head till morn?   you made it sound so easy
like a serious slut   a bit of a tramp   those rainy ghosts on
your windowpane remind you of lads you had again and again
their lips on your lips   which lips   you can't say   you trollop whore you don't
remember anymore   such a hussy Edna   the candle
burnt at both ends—hot wax on your tits? twat? what?   pretty kinky
no wonder you died the autumn of your life   think anyone gives a hoot
about a hooker's lonely trees   vanishing birds   loves that have come and come
enough with all the cum   you and your lost memory of them   you'd have liked
a bit more nookie   I'll bet Ms. hussy Millay liked to play   no judgment   I know you can't
reply   tart Edna   and I cannot say why   I'll take up your mantle   I'll be your
winter slut   I'll finish the job   hand blow rim   such lovely sins   I'll make winter sing
make old men cry again   I'll be your strumpet with the trumpet till the very end

Providence
Diana DeCesaris Champa

If you were looking, searching, I might suggest you walk down Main Street from the east bank of the river, up the hill that anchors the local art school to one of the city's colonial boulevards. To avoid the arduous walk up the asphalt mountain you need to cut through one of the secret passageways. These gangways do not show up on any maps, but their locations, peppered between Main and Benefit, have been passed down from generation to generation of residents, and occasionally to special visitors like yourself. This is the place where you cross paths with people who like the privacy of the passages. The middle-aged couple kissing and copping a feel on the set of stairs behind the theatre with sofas and film posters. Or you may come across someone on the leafy enclosure of the cement steps further on, the ones that lead to the back door of the gold bonnet bank. Or, just beside the museum, you might encounter an art student galloping down the iron set of steps hanging on to white plastic straws in the shape of the Star of Pegasus, the walls of facility threatening the sculpture's safety and student's grade for the class that started half an hour ago.

But none of these people interest you.

You pass them and move onto one of the most beautiful streets in the historic quarter where, because of the darkness brought on by the disruption of electricity, the streets are deserted and lit only with the old city's gas lights.

    You
        could have sworn
        that was the clock clop sound of horse steps ahead of you.

                Yes, that's what that sound is, it must be!

Looking behind you at the tall white steeple and the sandy brown, faded red and cornbread yellow wooden houses, you forget who you are, where you are and turn up the steps of one of the brick brownstones, skipping the lion head knocker and passing through the doorway, further into another year, another time, another life. Always as if for the first time, you cross the hall, its oak floor and panel walls silent as its cornices melt, greeting you warmly and massaging you towards the back staircase, the same stairs built for the hidden movement of servants between the floors. Your hand is lifted with a candle you don't remember picking up and a cold chill comes up and ruffles your dress, so you pick it up at the hem and the fabric around your thighs rustles as you walk up and up some more, each board and plank getting smaller as the walls tighten. You find yourself at the rooftop, at a window without a piece of glass. You lean out and, like me, find Providence.

A Box of Skyscrapers
Abigail Clarkin

How can words describe such a place
As this Providence...

Cold cutting through mittens as palms
Meet an icy rink?
Waterfire's heat and summer's
Humidity mixed—
A day in winter or July?

The scent of crepes and coffee grounds
In a small cafe,
Or the open, salted air of
A waterside park
On a windy day in April?

Hundred voices singing loudly
At outdoor concerts?
An induction ceremony
Proudly welcoming
Honor students in near silence?

Spikes against track as beautiful
As hand molded clay;
A display of speed at a state
Meet, or the patience
Shown at a ceramic art show?

There is no one sound or feeling
Or talent or place
That can make this capital
Into what it is
To all of those who have been here.

How can words even capture or
Contain a city?

People Don't Know
Wayne Renkin

People don't know there was a brook under my driveway
That went into the woods.
One day I followed it.
I found a rock as big as a two-story house.
The strange thing is
How did it get there
In the middle of the woods?

People don't know I want a woman.
People don't know that I have a vagus nerve stimulator under my skin
to stop seizures

For sure, people don't know I used to ride horses.
People don't know I raised 14 white-faced Herefords

People don't know there was dirt around my house
When it rained, the dirt turned into clumps.
When my sister came out of the house I would throw it up in the air and yell
 "Heads Up!"
and hit her in the head.

I used to ride my motorcycle on all the bike trails in the woods
And one day I opened that bike wide open
And that ramp hurled me 20 feet in the air.
I was flying, what can I say?
I felt free flying through the air
I can't say I felt like a bird
I don't know how birds feel
I wasn't afraid.
I was a 13-year-old flying desperado.

Impressions: Providence
Erin Perfect

impressions: providence
slatted light of the northern hemisphere
cast down blue
wood shingled silhouettes
a crisp line atmosphere
wind dirtying my collar
nuanced gusts, uniform waves
static across my ear.

Greetings from Providence, RI [4]

Purchased by Love
Mary Ann Mayer

Chief Canonicus of the Narragansett People gave Roger Williams the gift of land to found Providence. Williams later wrote: "Money could not have purchased Rhode Island. Rhode Island was purchased by love".

On the capitol dome of the littlest state,
gold-leafed, flood-lit,
a rogue stands
on faith.

Rogue on a marble dome,
in puritan boots and super-hero cape, surveys
the cityscape—one arm outstretched, trident raised
over the spread of Providence—

the Biltmore, hurricane barrier and bay,
the Superman building, vacant and soot-stained—
beneath him, black Amtrak-stitched snow
and traffic snakes,

bumper-to-bumper, down off-ramps to
under-passes, where people wait,
huddled and cold, on gritty streets named:
Empire, Benevolent, Friendship, Prospect, and Hope.

Too many make a gridlock of need,
too many people distressed,
too many palms outstretched,
entreat the headlights —for help to make ends meet,

for some kind of break, from the gridlock
of no paycheck, no prospect,
no providence, no hope.
But few cars stop.

So many have forgotten
the symbol of Rhode Island is the anchor of hope.
Or, never knew why Roger Williams wrote:
Rhode Island was purchased by love.

No, this down-turned time in the littlest state,
this drought of hope, has gone on so long—
who's numbered or blessed, who's hungry or fed,
who gets heat, a bed, a living wage,

feels like fate—the cards you're dealt—
to have nowhere to go, besides wait.
Nowhere to turn, besides look up
from the headlights, up

to the flood-lights,
to our hero-rogue standing on faith—
while pigeons and magistrates strut, unrustled,
and the dome's marble veins bleed out gray.

Still, the streets resound with prayers for rain.
Man, make it rain.
Rain down some love.
Make it a downpour.
Make it a hurricane.

Sheraton Biltmore Hotel in hurricane [5]

Missing Providence

Wendy Grossman

For the past four years, I have been creating daily found poems from weaving together lines from my friends' Status Updates on Facebook. Here are five of those poems that speak to me of our divine Providence.

east side nosh
perfect providence
snowpocalypse breakfast
coffee from
coffee exchange,
bagle/lox/whitefish salad
from davis
no mail
will be
delivered today
might as well dance

breeze hog
1) people I love
2) fighting for justice
voy a reir! voy a bailar!
while all you people
were slacking
punch punch duck
didn't think the
asphalt was that hot
sweltering summer lilies
outside of my office
little compton is
hoggin all the
breeze today
cooling down with
some dandies
I long for
70 degree weather
I stop drinking but I
still go to the bar

provy postcard
hello. you're welcome,
have a nice day
maybe I'm a
different breed,
blame it on
my a.d.d.
a diva since I
entered the world
I'm drinking some
chai tea thinking about
taking up tai chi
(literally. look!)
me and my favorite guy
completely. bald.
he's elated, and
I'm now dead inside
car semi-clean,
time to chill
this is someone's
house and yard
but then you go to
Cranston for fresh
donuts
privilege has it's
privileges
I love you all.

mount hope haiku
the majestic owl
really sick buick on cypress st.
there is no straight line

angel ray
bird on a rooftop
the waters at
your neck
the dancing cop
has returned
angel ray comes
to me with
$9 in cash
I ask her 15 questions
then I walk away
if you never dunked,
you won't understand
how difficult this is
not so melodic,
but the determined
tweeting of
little warblers
I couldn't identify
from discord,
find harmony
this is so beautiful
who knew

Contributors: Thanks to Jon Albert, April Aubrey, Shelby Baz, Bc Chronicles, Deni Yvan Béchard, Les Brooks, Denise Byrd, Vickie Canale, Davey Jay Clay, Larisa Colantonio, Rodney L Davis, Miriam Gilbert, Go Providence, Humans of New York, Nancy J. Jacobs, Christopher Johnson, Donald King, Melissa Potter Laundry, Warren Leach, Mary K O'Connor, Joe Pascone, Andrew Posner, Beth Ricci, RISD Museum, Chris Kazi Rolle, Angel Rosa, Shannon Rosa, Mark Santow, Jay Say, Medalit Scott, Nelson Taylor, Baratunde Thurston, Adrienne A Wallace, Eric Ward, Necie White, and Brian Wright.

Lighteater (pt. 2 of ∞)
Nicholas E. Morley

1. When Charles and Momoi first slept together it was first semester of sophomore year at Brown on a picnic blanket under citymuted stars on the roof of a riverfront Providence warehouse that failed four times:
- shipment storage, d. 1827 after the Rhode Island gradual-emancipation law of 1784 made slave laborers full citizens at 21 and the costs of living wages put the owner under,
- wool mill, d. 1930 due to the American Viscose Company's untimely monopoly and expansion of rayon production and its subsequent complete disembowelment of the East Coast textiles market,
- paper pulp treatment facility, d. 1982 in the financial scorched-earth of mounting a legal defense against the state's claim, later substantiated, that the firm misled a cadre of city trashmen (whose repeated naming by their legal counsel as "The Trashmen" led two of them to start a cover band with the plea deal cash) into dumping waste chemicals in the bay,
- and finally Seethe Nightclub, d. 2005 after Bill O'Reilly mentioned it offhand as a cathedral of utter sin "and perhaps a MOSQUE though," he added slyly with his chin shaking, "[he] wouldn't know one if [he] saw one," so local senior-citizen fundamentalists nightly duct-taped themselves to the doors weeping openly as they recited verses from Revelations in very declasse Salvo-acquired 1980's business casualwear—

which, really, Charles said into the soft crook of Momoi's stretched neck, was probably the reason folks stayed away and the place shuttered. The fashion? Momoi said and Charles nodded, The fashion. All the light browns and oranges and creams, I mean, it's a nightclub. He rubbed his eyes. Like writing Arbeit Macht Frei on a Viagra bottle.

Momoi sat up and stole a swig from the flask that had laid next to Charles' side of the blanket, spectator to their coupling. And here I thought I wouldn't find a boyfriend at this place, Momoi said. You shouldn't be drinking, said Charles and she laughed. Aren't you on antidepressants, said Charles and she laughed. Look, just, no, I don't want to go again, can we stop and talk about this, said Charles and she laughed. I'm fine, she said. You make me happy.

Charles asked if they could each go to their separate dorms because really it was pretty late and classes, you know. They buttoned their respective skinny jeans in silence and faced opposite vistas: Charles, the sweep of the Providence River delta with its dual bridges and foundries and empty timeshare houseboats at harbor, docked promises for freedom at a low monthly rate reminding him to work on his History of Architecture midterm; and Momoi, the brick sprawl up one shoulder of College Hill, the lights behind apartment shutters, the wafts of music from house parties, happy social people she'd yet to meet and, with this latest rejection, dreaded she'd never become. The key was other people—no, or, she was certain, or, if her parents taught her anything, at least she thought she knew—the key could not be her.

2. Charles stopped his antidepressants in high school. It was the Czech Republic and the stuff they used was old, nasty tricyclics from back when anti-psychotics could kill as soon as cure. They were interfering with enjoying his classes and getting out. Everything was flat then, he said. Nothing had its grooves.

He didn't tell his parents when he stopped. If he had they would have stuck them in his daily morning oatmeal. Cigarettes were his go-to soother for the post-med shakes since pot was expensive and made it hard to focus on school, which he loved without question.

One evening after his study group agreed they'd internalized chemistry sufficient to pass the midterm they drove to a lake that was once a town. It had been flooded by the Soviets just before the Velvet Revolution. All the roadsigns indicating the town's existence had been changed so they had to puzzle their way through a foldout map from 1962 before they found it.

A road broke through treelimbs weighted with moss and led to the water, dove down where no car would follow. They swam out to the steeple of a church, tilted white finger alone on the surf, and sat on the roof while the oldest of the five taught them all how to roll their own smokes, tobacco and cloves pinched from plastic bags sealed with duct-tape. This was the grooves. Charles smoked two and made jokes about the end of all things looking like this. The rising sea levels, our cityscapes gone the way of Venice. Another Biblical flood and even now, even with all that's been done, we would not survive. Water, great solvent, ever-cleanser.

A girl Charles had dated and broke up with in middle school dared him to dive deep in the water and as he took off his wet shirt to do so he slipped on the mildewed church roof's shingles and went in legs-first, eyes open.

In the heavy murk and paintflecks like snowflakes he was suspended and timeless. This was the grooves. Homes crushed by water pressure, himself deweighted, his t-shirt floating to the surface and just behind it the bubbles of his breath headed to the moon. Hair in his eyes. Branches for fingers. Below, somewhere, failed architecture. He still journals about this moment as his brief brush with transcendence, something his move to America, to Providence, has yet to bring. Mute bliss. Peopleless.

3. Momoi went to a private middle and high school down the road from her childhood home in a somnolent tree-ridden suburbia full of doctors and doctors' lovers off the Massachusetts elbow of I-495. She was diagnosed by the school's in-house psychiatrist with Major Depressive Disorder when she was 12 and given Abilify, then Celexa.

She became fluent in Korean at 13 and French at 16.

She invited five friends for her 17th birthday and two came.

Her grades were stellar.

She made breakfast before school, before her parents woke. Two eggs, with ketchup, one English muffin, with butter, and one glass of milk, with Nesquik chocolate mix, laid out before her precise as watchworks, she would stare out the kitchen window at the road and its flanking thicket bocage for half an hour.

The National Honors Society made her president her senior year.

When she went to bed it would take her two good book chapters to fall asleep and then in the night she would wake sopped with sweat and with heart at a sprint shivering her ribcage.

Her teachers gushed in P-T meetings. Her parents (father anesthesiologist, mother baker) were gently supportive and encouraged her to follow her dreams though vaguely and without prescription and when anything seemed to be slipping gave her the old Shame Upon Your Family routine and then offered to watch a DVR'd episode of Saturday Night Live together to get across their united front of care.

The first night she smoked marijuana and drank hard liquor was the same night and she was 15 and she stood weak-kneed at the summit of a hill overlooking the stretched-long Minuteman National Park with her nine classmates hunkered on mossed rocks as they all watched their illegal bonfire all simmers and pops and melted covers of old New Yorkers and she could not tear her gaze from the ink-tint flames.

She was a co-captain for varsity tennis junior and senior years and ran cross-country in the fall.

Girls talked of boys' talks of wanting her and she kissed them, girls and boys, sometimes and their brief romances were reserved to the realms of texts and class parties (always held at Lancie McClane's place, a lesser mansion, Gatsby-esque with iPod playlists) and in them she found whole new wide avenues of self-evaluation and terror and the unknown and though the joy of care and sex shone through in pinpoints the existential weight of self-reflection via her love for others extinguished chances at connection.

She volunteered at the soup kitchen run out of the Unitarian Church and wore disposable gloves to shake poor people's hands.

When she walked to school sometimes and the light was the right shade of gray she could detach and watch Her, grounded, on the road, backpacked, on the march and feel her Self, afloat, get caught on the winds over the treeline and whisked somewhere distant and warm though soon there she was again caught in that vessel of flesh being honked at by a stopped 18-wheeler on a tight corner where she was an obstacle (there were no sidewalks).

She played a level-headed jazz piano when she wanted to, had time, got roped into the floundering high school jazz band to back up the other instruments on their concert nights on occasion.

She was accepted to MIT, Middlebury, Brown, Cornell, and Northeastern and though Northeastern offered a hefty scholarship Brown seemed the most free and she'd come to value that which she had least of, freedom: moments most open to possibility, long rooms of time in which she could breathe.

By senior year she had 847 Facebook friends, 27 Twitter followers, and 17 Tumblr frequent-rebloggers and her college essays were well-composed and made frequent use of quotes from the works of Nelson Mandela and Malcolm X and her hands, spiderish and calloused, had weight written at their ends, nails frayed, bitten, jigsawed.

These were her gives.

4. The last time Charles and Momoi slept together was spring semester of junior year after Momoi knocked on Charles' door and as he opened it she tumbled forward with her hands on his chest sending them sprawling to the lowset twin bed

and with vodka on her breath and cheeks flush she pressed her face into his and ground herself against his right thigh and slipped her hand down his sweatpants and gripped the shaft of his limp penis and when Charles knocked her hand away and shouted Stop she, straddling him, wept. She said, I just don't want to be depressed anymore. I want it to stop. Won't you let me? Won't you give me that? Won't you just—

Charles cradled her as the sobs doubled her over, then tugged her to his left onto the open sliver of bed, their bodies mismatched parentheses. He sang Radiohead songs until she fell asleep.

At 4 AM she woke and slid out of bed and he woke but didn't show it and watched her sit and shake her head and comb her hair with her fingers and shake her head and comb faster until she left.

He texted her his desire to speak again and the general wish that she be well. Her reply took four months, postponed by a gnawing sense of misplaced value in others as pertained to her self-worth that tossed her in her sleep and kept her mouth shut at parties and drove her to books and movies and speaker events and nights spent staring at the fine geometric layout of her desk with the pill bottles stiff at the corners like orange see-through rooks. The text she eventually sent read, I will be well, have a nice life.

Time slowed as she adjusted to alcoholless existence. Her days stretched, molassesesque, each moment more agonizingly emotionally taxing than the last. Her writing assignments and reports grew tumorous with vigor. Her friendships, cruxed on shared imbibing, fell apart. She stopped buying physical books and instead pirated .pdfs and her savings account and laptop's hard drive simultaneously swelled. She watched a documentary on Netflix every morning. She picked up a fifty-cent copy of Leaves of Grass. She made folders within folders within her Firefox bookmarks folder.

If she consumed the world whole perhaps, when her equation balanced out, she'd end up on the right side of all things. Perhaps then she would be of worth. Perhaps, soon, she could reach something approaching good.

5. Charles knew none of this and experienced, for the first time, a social amputation, for the most part clean.

After Momoi, Charles experienced stretches of flirtation, but the connections were unfamiliar—what slavish sense of dependency for personal validation she'd felt for him had become the core emotion around which he structured his own affections, and so he flocked to those that intimated as such toward him in his social circles—yet he also, however unconsciously, was aware of the endgame of such a relational dynamic, Momoi's drunken pleas for release having become a recurring nightmare. Thus he found himself both attracted and repulsed from lust, his momentum lost by the end of pleasantries like a ball's bounce halving itself. He'd bring over drinks only to down his, say he had to piss, and leave the bar. He'd ask a woman's name, nod, turn on his heel and meld into the crowd. He'd pose the first part of a joke, stop, gape, blink his eyes a little, observe each waiting face as if they were some sort of predator looking for an in, a good place to bite him, a moment of weakness to pounce on, and he'd say, The Aristocrats (or something similarly conclusive in a catch-all panaceatic way) and promptly walk away.

That was what he'd become, he thought: a panacea, too timid to threaten or attract, that support that holds the hull together that nobody knows the name of.

To sooth this constant sense of inner entropy he spent his free time between classes learning old blues standards, reflecting on the infinities of past sadness born from the crooked foundation of America, that jilted idealist, and occasionally reading the Bible or Vonnegut.

He walked out to India Point Park one Saturday night with his Gibson acoustic and watched the surf eat at the supports of harbors left marooned in the bay, ancient hallmarks of the still-used name: Rhode Island and Providence Plantations. "It's dark and it's raining and I've got to go home, got to go home, boys, got to go home," he sang to the sea.

He had exams coming. He had to call his parents. He had to check his loans. He had to see a family friend applying to Brown that was visiting tomorrow. He had to pay rent. He had to pick up shifts with the catering crew. People, commitments, like a shifting web with him tied taut to its center, the strands made of the metal of chainlink fences, rusted and biting his wrists and ankles. He missed suspension, gravityless abandon in the water in that flooded town, wasted place, lost to history.

Here he was though, at the reins of his own uncharted course, in full control, like it or not. He held the only key to his floodgates. He could open them, or not, or thrive. To become a ghost-town or midsize metropolis? Emptiness, he concluded, was a temptation, an easy out, a nice thing to see to know it's there and not much else.

He had not come to Providence the easy way, nor had many who called it home. He stopped playing guitar and took from his back pocket a flask and drank it dry and finished the song. "It's dark and it's raining and I've got to go home, I'm on my long journey home."

Silent Meeting: 2015
Adele Bourne

White-haired men, women, a grandchild on the facing bench.
Heads bowed. Some asleep. Girls in bright dresses.
Tiny Rosie, as usual, in her pajamas.
Blue- jeaned siblings, boyfriends in their first beards.
Malcontent three year-old carried out to the nursery.
Upper gallery filled with modest ghosts.
Through the tall windows , new leaves on century-old trees.
At the feeders made by the First Day School,
Goldfinches, robins, orioles.
Banners flap: "Drone Free Zone,"
(Don't Go, Don't Go , Don't Go, Don't Go)
Out on the lawn black pinwheels spin,
One for each child killed last summer:
"Muhammed Aba' Khan, aged 2 ½."

Aftermath, 2013
Sienna Zeilinger

The first thing I do when I hear about the bombing is call my roommate, whose family lives in Cambridge. The tenth thing I do is arrive at a cemetery.

The eighth thing: Get on my bike and pedal aimlessly. The ninth: Decide on north. The place I have in mind backs up against the Seekonk River, and I've heard you can see ducks there.

On the first Tuesday of third grade, we were told that some bad guys had crashed some planes into some buildings. "We aren't close," my teacher said. Our vocabulary word that week was "inherit." The seventh thing I do is throw the damn potatoes away.

Fifth: Take out my phone and Google "empathy." Sixth: Delete my browser's history.

Fourth: Congregate for a late lunch. We are an hour away from Boston. I'm from the Midwest, and I haven't yet lived in Providence two years, and so I measure distance in terms of time and find a visceral sort of comfort in the potatoes on my plate. Our table is square and sticky and across from the cafeteria's cereal station. I watch a freshman look from Cheerios to Cinnamon Toast Crunch to Cheerios again; Alexander watches the TV. CNN is showing the younger brother's face. "I smoked with that guy," Alexander says. The freshman decides on Wheaties, and Alexander puts down his fork. "We went to high school together. I've sat in his car."

Before that: Recall that a human heart is the size of a closed fist.

And before that: Say, "You okay?"

The rain falls lightly and sideways. The ducks, it turns out, are swans. I take off my helmet and hold it in my hands and try not to cry.

We Are Providence
Nada Samih Rotondo

*"She came from Providence,
the one in Rhode Island
Where the old world shadows hang
heavy in the air
She packed her hopes and dreams
like a refugee
Just as her father came across the sea"
- The Eagles, The Last Resort*

Each section of the city of Providence holds magic for me. Mount Pleasant is home to some of the only old growth oaks in the city, Federal Hill's original Narragansett name is Nocabulabet, which means place between the ancient waters, and Fox Point was a major international shipping center, with slave ships and all. While the sycamores, forgotten bridges, and the layers of history are fair game for any artist searching for inspiration, Providence has burrowed her way into my dislodged center, setting it right again. She has made me feel at home against all odds.

Growing up Palestinian in Rhode Island, my need for relevance and connection was fierce. While undoubtedly this is connected to Palestine's longing for statehood and international recognition, it's also because Rhode Island is not an easy place to immigrate to. Directions are impossible to deal with unless you happen to know "where the old Dunkin Donuts used to be." Sometimes the same road has several different route numbers and locations are referred to by their "unofficial" name. No, South County is not an actual county.

I never set foot in Palestine, but with my Teta's grandmother stories I at least got to feel like I did. I know the fishermen and orange grooves in Yaffa well enough to imagine the sights and sounds of our ancestral land. I remember her countless retellings of that ill fated spring in 1948, with it's thunderous bombings and dismembered bodies vividly enough to feel as though I witnessed them myself. While my grandmother's stories were already seeding my identity, my own experience with fleeing Kuwait as a six year old added to the entanglement of roots.

Missing Providence

My mother and I fled Kuwait a few weeks after the Iraqi invasion in 1990. Despite the whirlwind of narrowly escaping plundering soldiers, intense desert heat, and a custody battle that included a thumb-less kidnapper hired by my father's family (a story for another day), I was thrown into this new world without so much as a guidebook. In elementary school while my classmates ate peanut butter jelly sandwiches, I ate Zaet and Zaatar pita my mom packed. In second grade you could easily spot me in the school cafeteria. I was that girl with the frizzy braids and thick rimmed pink glasses (before they were cool), patiently explaining in broken English that no, I wasn't eating bird poop, just herbs mixed with olive oil.

My mother, finally freed from stifling gender norms, could raise me without fear. Since she was divorced, it was law that I would only be with her till age eleven, after which my father—a distant but not wholly unpleasant accountant, would have been my legal guardian. Had my mother remarried or been caught out on a date, she would be deemed an unfit mother, losing custody even sooner, perhaps even securing my fate as a math whiz instead of a writer.

As the months grew into years, the novelty of Rhode Island faded. I hungered after stability in people and places. I envied my classmates for the simple routines that involved sport practices or family vacations. While they went along their seasonal routines, in my family there was still talk of moving away, of new schools, new relationships, and yet another world to get accustomed to. I ached for a predictable life. I still find myself in awe of people who have the notion that life will unfold in exactly the same way it had for generations. I knew the comfort was an illusion. I understood that friends had some flavor of childhood trauma or economic insecurity rippling beneath the placid surface of their day-to-day lives, but I envied the illusion. My experiences were too raw to be hidden. They had marked me with a discordant vibration, amplified by the cadence of my mispronounced name. I recognize this discordance in others. In fact, Providence is abuzz with it; all those layers of old world muck latticed through downtown's polished center. You can see it in people and places like the half-collapsed Moshassuck bridge; centuries old, dark in the shadow of newly constructed luxury condominiums. My insecurities mirrored by the city itself.

I might not have fit in where I wanted to, but at least Providence understands. I could never experience home in the same way my Teta did, but I could lean on Providence for support. Like so many before me, I have been seduced by this haven for those "distressed for conscience," and I'd like to think that it's no mere coincidence. While researching the role of State Pier One's role in immigration for a story idea, I came across some surprising information: The Fabre Line, a fleet of steamships, supplied Providence with immigrants well into the twentieth century. Immigration quotas threatened to put the Fabre Line out of business, but they decided to redirect the routes and pick up immigrants and visitors from cities like Beirut, Alexandria and Yaffa. Yaffa! The same city my family was forced to flee in 1948. This steamship came from Providence and went to Yaffa as part of it's journey, to pick up goods and people way back before my disoriented self ever stood on that Providence pier. Could it be that after several years of defining myself as a misplaced and misunderstood outcast, I had actually been home in Providence after all? Do I have ancestors floating around having a good laugh, chuckling 'oh silly girl! nothing is random.'?

I remember downtown before the mall, before Water Place Park and well before those luxury towering condos. The tourism council will have you thinking that Providence always had a glowing face of fancy restaurants and Waterfire, but I knew her before the Botox injections. Before she tried to hide her puffy post-industrial eyes and walk in Boston's high-heeled pumps. Maybe if we sit by the Providence River at dusk and look down toward the smoke stacks and consider the gentle lapping of its briny water, we could hear the voices that came before us. If we hold still and listen closely, we might even hear H. P. Lovecraft famously proclaim, I am Providence. To which we can now respond: "No Mr. Lovecraft. We are Providence".

PART II

ENCOUNTERS

Christian Hill
Janaya Kizzie

When I stepped out of the Hoyle the sound dropped away, and the cold winter wind was cupping the flush in my cheeks and I admit I was drunk and thinking, rich men are criminals. There was the sound of metal creaking in the wind, but the voices from the inn were mostly gone, though there was laughter and singing.

The world burns me, and I am feeling my drink.

If I stay here, the snow would wrap me up like her infant son, and the city would walk on. The whores on Benefit would still laugh and sing, and the Point would still fill with bodies. You and I, rich and poor, would stand, older than the obelisks, like figures frozen in a photograph. The white wind would tear through the stillness, and we, still and black, would peer blurrily into time.

We would watch one another forever.

Old Hoyle Tavern formerly at junction of Westminster & Cranston St. [7]

"Bella Apocalypse,"
Adele Bourne

 She called me.
My name for her?
" Ebola Ann."

See that squirrel in the pear tree?
Four litters in a year. We were luckier.
—Hey, jump! He's after you. —
 She gave me this nature book
 just before she left.
No wonder squirrels are so hungry.

 No. I' m not going back.
I saw Satan in the bathroom.

Oh, strawberry, please. Look.
Same color as her prom dress. Remember?
The one you gave me. The year she wore it,
Varsity Hotshot, "Every Mother's Dream,"
Slipped her the rough stuff, helped her on her way.

She didn't know. He didn't tell her. No one ever
Told you. Maybe scared you'd kill him.
Burn down the school. Yes, I'm fine.
The Oasis of Grace keeps me safe.
 Elder gave me this Bible. He says one day
I'll see my son, sooner or later.

 At Chapel we pray for the Marines.
 Remember Tommy? They're flying out
Somewhere tomorrow.
Silence not enough, not any more.
I love this outdoor café.
You always were my favorite teacher.

J-Coby Wayne

PASSAGE
Wealth and poverty uneasy bedfellows
as lives pass to and fro
under the high vaulted ceiling
lit by surreal orange light.

Direction and directionless,
hope and despair waiting side by side
as the bedraggled man begs
and the young Marine waits—
to go off to his imaginary war.
As he smiles an innocent smile,

the beggar stares vacantly
with lost eyes and nowhere to go,
nothing to grasp to himself—
not even an imaginary war.

As the night deepens
and the orange lights
become more surreal,
the last train pulls out,
leaving behind the desperate men.

THE MUSEUM

The two of you sit
In a room that is too hot.
Surrounded by a quiet love story
captured in mostly black + white.

I experience a love so profound
it cannot be defined.
Traditional labels seem so inane,
so stupid.
You both seem so frail
in a shocking, unexpected way.

Standing above,
I see thinning hair a metaphor for
the passage of time.
But time stands still

+ runs backward
+ runs ahead so fast,

I know I could have been on some bench
somewhere –
needing to rest –
at an unexpected moment not
so far in the future.

From a Detroit-born camera
from the 1930s,
I see my Hungarian grandfather looking out
at me
in a 2008 Rhode Island exhibit hall,
+ lines that separate, blur.

Eleanor,
I find myself some peace in you.
A body thickening over time,
but your gaze so direct,
so simple, so knowing,
so uncomplicated by doubt.

The father I thought would be
forever strong,
curled in on himself
like a Harry Callahan leaf
ready to blow away.

The mother I perceived in youth
as weak,
the rock.
The strong one.
The one who found her voice
only to lose her speech.

She will find it again.

They are so beautiful to me
in that moment,
so precious.
More beautiful than they
ever were in youth.

The gift of life + love, it seems,
only possible with the passage
of time, that mortality,
that tide of changing places.

Love wrapped in moments
tender
that take you by surprise
on those little cat feet.

On Empire Street
Mary Ann Mayer

After a nice dinner at Bravo
of monkfish and a fifty-dollar un-oaked Chardonnay,
I'm parked at the curb this hot August night
ready to blow another fifty up my nose,

when this guy staggers over,
scabs on his lips, clenched fists for eyes.
I slip the lines, the mirror and rolled up dollar bill under my thigh,
locking the door as he lurches toward me, yelling,

"Hey can you just give me two quarters?
I need a bus so I can go home. I just got out of the hospital.
 Come on, two quarters is all."

I roll up my windows fast
and can't recall exactly, but think I yelled back something like,
"Can you just stop goddamn yelling at me?"

What would you do?
Give him the quarters?

If I thought he had a job
If he wasn't standing ankle deep in empties
If his wounds weren't fresh out of years of mistakes
If his heart was unruined
If he wasn't a junkie
If he looked anything like me
If he looked anything like Jesus
If a clap of thunder and a cross on a hill. If lightning forked the sky
If passersby weren't staring…

      …If only my car window was painted black
but then it would turn into a mirror, then
my reflection, and
who needs that?

Always be the same amount
Alexander Smith

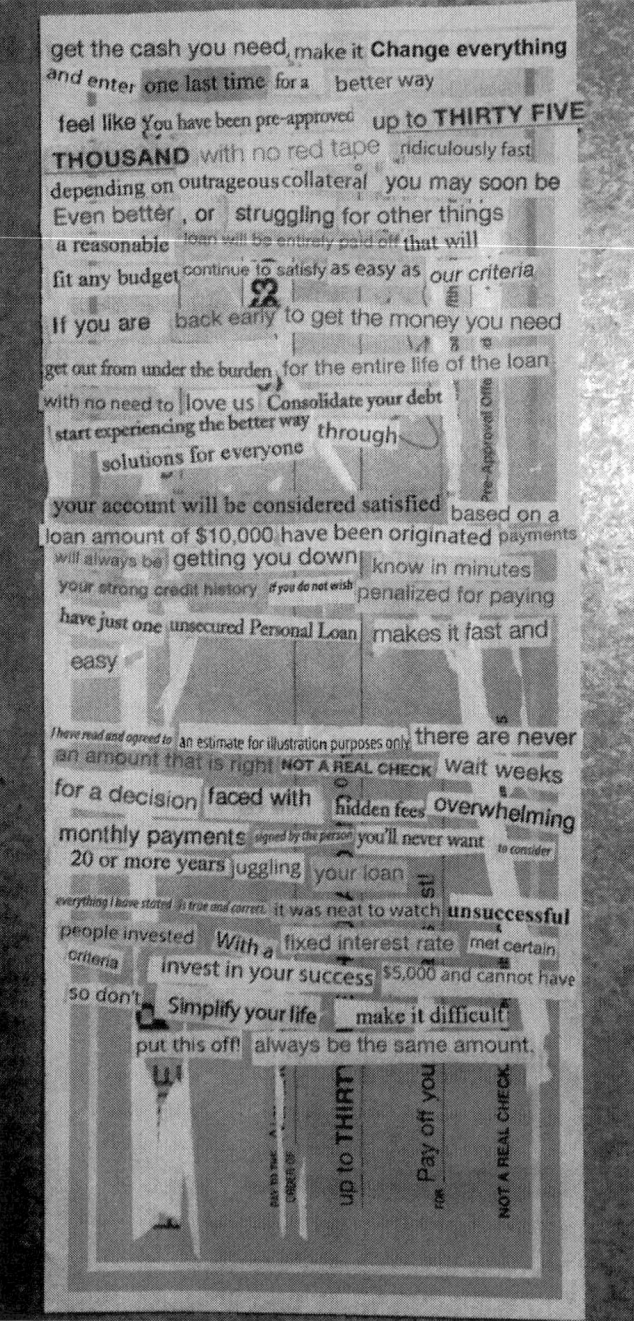

Missing Providence

Old Mills & Cheap Rent
Dan Shewan

The first thing I see is the faces. They stand watch over the highway, promising wine and cars and justice. They smile, teeth bared in thirty-foot grins, but I don't trust them. They follow me around the city, their eyes watching me from bus stops and off-ramps, their hollow promises masquerading as concern.

We keep going, the detritus of our past packed into corrugated cardboard boxes scrawled with black Sharpie, piled high in the back of the U-Haul that will carry us to our new life. We pass old mills that, like the faces, have seen their city slowly change, their smokestacks dormant, their windows broken. Cinder block strip clubs and warehouses cling to the highway, huddled beneath telephone wires and power cables, faded awnings torn, vinyl banners flapping in the breeze like flags.

This is where I will be understood. This is where the words will come easily and the looks of people passing me in the street will be recognition, of acceptance, not the blank, empty selfishness of the suburbs. This is where I will belong.

*

During our occasional visits to Providence before we moved here, my wife and I would take long walks around College Hill, enviously admiring the pristine Victorian homes that lined the quiet, leafy streets. I imagined the life we could live here. I pictured myself walking down these streets, my satchel filled with books, on my way to a coffee shop where I would effortlessly write revealing, insightful essays and thoughtful short stories that would be published by prestigious literary journals. In the evenings, we would eat at one of the city's many restaurants, sampling cuisine from around the world, discussing art and urgent social problems. We would browse the shelves at the Brown Bookstore on Thayer and talk about important books with the clerks. We would attend exhibitions at the RISD galleries, purchase our groceries from farmers markets and independently owned, socially responsible coops, support local businesses at craft fairs.

I would love nothing more than to say that it was Providence's artistic community that drew us here, to serve as living proof that a visible commitment to the arts attracts new residents, creates new opportunities, and drives sustainable, long-term growth.

The real reason we moved here is because the rent is cheap.

It would be a grave disservice to say Providence's cultural qualities weren't a contributing factor in our decision. However, the city's affordable rental market was the single most important factor in our choice to move here. We had endured the rapidly increasing cost of living in the metro Boston area for several years, and having finally been priced out of even the city's most homogenous, culturally sterile suburbs, found ourselves in desperate need of a more affordable – and agreeable – place to live. I was working as a copywriter for a software startup in Boston and needed to take the train from Providence to Back Bay five days a week. My wife had finally quit her demanding teaching job to focus on her own art. While we both love the atmosphere and sense of community in Providence dearly, price and logistical feasibility triumphed over romanticized idealism.

Prior to moving here, my wife and I were largely unaware of the $100,000 rebranding campaign Providence underwent in 2009 that resulted in its new moniker of "The Creative Capital." Shortly after we had settled into our modest apartment in the West End, I read an archived news article about former mayor Cianci's vocal opposition to the budget allocated to the rebranding. Despite Cianci's juvenile remarks about the financial investment, it seems to be paying off. Art has become a prominently visible part of the city's landscape, the sides of dusty red brick buildings transformed into vast, vivid canvasses. The inaugural Providence International Arts Festival appeared to be a tremendous success, proving that a city-wide commitment to the arts can unite communities and revitalize downtown districts once thought forsaken.

However, the cultural "renaissance" (to borrow Cianci's glib term for the city prior to its rebranding) that Providence is undergoing is both encouraging and deeply disconcerting.

Art in Providence is something that people make. Art in Boston is something that people sell. The passion for true creation evident throughout Providence's artistic community is something that Boston, with its preoccupation with the blood sport of pandering to the rich and powerful, could never hope to emulate. While the arts have proven a force to be reckoned with in Providence's renewal, its future is far from guaranteed. Cultural capital can indeed transform cities and shape communities – but the costs can be high, a valuable lesson that the city could learn well from Boston.

The purpose of any artistic investment at a civic level is to increase revenue, primarily through tourism. A disproportionately small amount of money for programs like the Providence International Arts Festival comes from taxpayers; the vast majority of it comes from corporate donors and sponsors. This forces policymakers to enter into a Faustian bargain. On one hand, corporate concerns are uniquely positioned to further the arts in cities like Providence. On the other, the infusion of corporate funding means that artistic organizations are subject to the whims of their boardroom benefactors. Boston embraced the arts-as-marketing paradigm enthusiastically with its Literary Cultural District, a program that offered little benefit to anyone besides the already privileged white writers fortunate enough to live and work in the city, and owners of the already prized and wildly expensive real estate within the District itself. I cannot help but wonder if Providence's artistic community will eventually be packaged and sold in a similar fashion.

Another question that remains unanswered is how the city's focus on the arts will create jobs or, indeed, whether it should. It is inevitable that some jobs will be created as a result of the city's continued investment in cultural programs, but for the most part, this is little more than a byproduct of attempts to part tourists from their money. Events like the Providence International Arts Festival won't help the long-term unemployed learn new skills, or create jobs in sufficient numbers to reduce the city's stubbornly high unemployment rate. For out-of-state transplants such as my wife and I, the city's focus on the arts is highly alluring and makes Providence a wonderful place to live. For many residents, it is merely another failure of the Rhode Island General Assembly to take meaningful action to address wider, more urgent state-wide problems almost a decade in the making. To some, the Providence International Arts Festival might as well have taken place in another state for all the good it did them.

In some ways, perhaps it did.

Providence often reminds me of other former manufacturing hubs that have struggled to reconcile their rich and prosperous past with their uncertain present, such as Buffalo and Detroit. In many ways, Providence is virtually indistinguishable from the beleaguered cities of the Rust Belt. They feature the same distinctive blend of Art Deco and Beaux Arts architecture, share the same rich industrial manufacturing pasts, and have endured the same long, difficult struggles to redefine their identities in the new economy.

Of course, Providence possesses what cities like Buffalo and Detroit lack— world-class universities that attract academic talent from all over the world. The city has long been renowned as the home of Brown University, the Ivy League alma mater of cultural luminaries including writers Jeffrey Eugenides and Rick Moody, and Pulitzer-winning playwrights Lynn Nottage and Quiara Alegría Hudes, to name but a select few. The Rhode Island School of Design, Brown's equally esteemed neighbor, has also been long considered one of Providence's most valuable assets. Few cities in the Rust Belt can boast cultural and academic credentials of Providence's caliber, and it makes sense that the city would value creativity so highly.

However, while Providence has always attracted some of the brightest, most talented people in the world, it rarely manages to keep them. They come, study in and around historic College Hill, before leaving Rhode Island to achieve the pinnacles of accomplishment for which many of the alumni of these schools have become famous. Some choose to stay, but most are forgotten as soon as they cross state lines until they achieve the professional destinies for which Providence's prestigious colleges prepare them. Providence boasts a vibrant artistic and cultural community that would be the envy of many cities, but whether or not it can persuade the next generation of artists, writers, and scientists to remain here after donning their cap and gown remains doubtful.

The enduring problem of human capital flight is reflected by recent population forecasts for the city. Official estimates indicate that the population of Providence will stagnate for at least another fifteen years. Even in the 2030s, the city's marginal population growth – much of which is expected to be driven by the immigration of foreign nationals—will be offset by the number of projected deaths. While stability is preferable to decline, I wonder if the city's commitment to the arts can attract sufficient numbers of new artists and writers and performers, the way it attracted my wife and I, amid the challenges of the continually rising cost of living and a languid economy.

The last of the old mills and abandoned factories, the once-beating heart of the city that ran with the lifeblood of industry, will inevitably be renovated into luxurious loft apartments that few of the artists whose romanticized lifestyle will be coopted by marketing campaigns could ever hope to afford. The Providence International Arts Festival will undoubtedly become an annual tradition, but whether it can do so without sacrificing the very art it was created to celebrate for corporate gain remains to be seen. The city's developing neighborhoods, including my own adopted West End, will continue to change, transformed by the gradual influx of people seeking an affordable home like shorelines shaped by the tides, but many families who have lived here for generations will be forced out.

Regardless of what brought us here, whether artistic inspiration or affordable rent, I am proud to call Providence home. My evening strolls may take a different route than the ones I had envisioned along the leafy streets of College Hill, but my satchel is full of books, life is good, and the words are coming easily.

The only question is for how long.

Brown & Sharpe Mfg. Co. [9]

Ascending Without Orpheus:
~a Dip into RISD's Fountain
Ira Schaeffer

It's a mopey, drizzly April day turning ugly
with the sun. Birdie chirps, the mailman's whistling—
low-life crocuses exposing their gaudy bits
—it's all a melancholic's buzz kill.

A pestilence of airborne pheromones
is spreading its rash of giddiness,
fevered brains and throbbing heads—
oblivious to the anguish of love.

Fecund nature, I'm so tired
of your brutal tenderness, exhausted
by your spastic dance, and yet I wonder
if this season might be the last I'll hear
your sweet, sweet music.

I feel no stirring—no compulsion
to leergropehave every curvypert
mothersistergrannyaunt—no horns,
no pipes, or tambourines to rattle.

I might as well spend my days with Orpheus
stuck in a fount of dread. My love turned
to a pillar of death, my voice, my art twisted
by suffering— Only tragedy for me,
my song, a bleak telegram
that life … stop is pain … stop and …wait!

Look at those legs, that smile, those eyes–
my horns are sprouting. My cup
overflows—the old goat rises!

Quiet
by Kylie Wyman

Quiet.

She was when I first met her.

I spoke loudly with actions. Dancing wildly about her darker corners.

Desperate, it almost seemed, my attempts to reach out and touch her heart with inebriated love ballads.

But I did not know how to love her then.

I could not recognize her beauty, hiding under smoke and shame.

Quiet.

I was when she began sharing secrets with me.

And I could hear her through the sights she revealed.

Sights forming in the shape of figures. Glowing and growing in her brighter corners.

How silly to think I could truly love in my darkest corners.

How silly to almost deny myself this providence.

Providence River and harbor by night [10]

A.M. Anderson

A woman crossing Thayer St
barefoot and listening to the street
this Jane wearing Tarzan steps
through warm walls of July air

her gait a humid rising
under unkempt tresses unfolding
down opposite sides of her broad skull
and dissipate over her breasts—

Her eyes lock on some far corner
beyond which must lie home terrain—
what now holds her from bounding
across the trafficked street?

Periodically, she stops
by another tribe to ask the time
as if the needed answer
became lost somewhere
among other faces
and leaves

Before dinner, I stop at Coffee Exchange
coffee-stained nostrils
the reward for making it this far
from university to a fair trade cup of joe
out on the deck, the wrens are little beggars
inquisitive, brave crumb hunters—
among the books and glances
go the quiet ploys for connection
and the soft stratagems of summer
breezes, murmurs of peopled
conversations caught up in branches
of a late afternoon's feathered light

britomart, burgundy bicycle
Juli Anna J. Herndon

twin wheels of liberty,
witch's whisk. mabel, my mare,
blood chestnut, canary-and-white.

serpentine antlers,
thrust into woman's hands.

two, circular crank of summering

thighs. sleek beast tusks.
nod and blink, conspiracy,
camaraderie. secret lock-knots,
emblem of agency; twinned twins.

equine ears pricked, mirrored
pupils. fierce. bubble of steel tubes and bodies.

imaginary squealof tires
or a whinney with impunity up.

Planted For Spring
C.A.Demi

The potatoes buried at the bottom of the bin felt like corpses' heels and elbows. Small bits of earth clung in the sockets of their eyes. When I withdrew my hand and dropped the potato I'd chosen into my basket, my fingers were left soiled. The potatoes on top were just as cold, just as foreign feeling, so there was no reason for rooting to the bin's bottom other than my being distracted. Cara had come to the market. She'd started at the opposite end of the half circle of vendors and bought a bag of carrots from a farmer from Massachusetts. Drawing up another potato, I watched her move to the next table where she selected a wreath of dried, flowering mugwort stems. She held it to her face. As she inhaled the wreath's fragrance, I could see her shoulders rise and fall despite their being covered by both an oversized fleece jacket and a voluminous silk scarf—the latter of which was the last gift I'd given her, a gesture too inadequate to compensate for the thing from me she'd most wanted. After paying for the flowers, Cara walked across the patch of schoolyard grass, around which the farmers' tents and tables were arranged, to confront me directly. As she approached I began selecting potatoes, with both hands, from the top of the bin, and continued to do so even as she came to a stop and stood over me. I could offer no more than a weak, dying sigh in response to her greeting. Nor could I bring myself to lift my gaze above her knees until she asked about my grandmother.

The halyard tinged against the vacant flagpole in front of the high school. The latch of a farmer's van clacked and its door opened. I could smell the mugwort looped over Cara's arm as well as the cool loam from which the potatoes had been exhumed. I considered telling her my grandmother had died. It wasn't true, but I wanted Cara to think her moving out wasn't still the worst thing that had happened. I wanted to turn her compassion against her. I wanted to lie just for the sake of lying. It wouldn't have mattered. Cara's gift had always been seeing the truth of my false smiles and my feigned frowns. Instead, the lie about my grandmother remained planted deep within me. Cara said a few other things—about her new apartment, about how unlikely it was that we hadn't more frequently chanced to see each other. I said something about how I got lost every time I went to the Westside. She was trying to be nice, to show me, by example, how we could remain on pleasant terms. I couldn't any longer look in her direction. I peered into my basket and, realizing that I'd taken more than intended, tossed the biggest, dirtiest potatoes back into the bin.

After we spoke, Cara went to the cheese stand. She embraced the girl in the red coat who worked there—and with whom, in spite of myself, I looked forward to having a brief transaction every week. I hadn't known the girl in the red coat and Cara to be so close, but the girl held Cara and patted her back for a long time. When the embrace ended, their hands remained on each others sides. Flower duff, loosened from the wreath by the contact of their bodies, lofted into the breeze.

Again Cara's shoulders rose and fell. She sobbed.

The farmer from whom I was buying the potatoes clutched the money I'd given him and thrust his hand toward me. I hadn't paid enough. The farmer watched closely as I dug up another wadded dollar from my jeans. Without saying a word, he was telling me that if I wanted a hug, or any kind of consolation, I'd need to find it somewhere else.

In the spring the market will reopen at its new location, Lippitt Park, whose playground and tended open spaces will entice more families to bring out their strollers and make an event of their shopping. In the spring the potato farmer will sell bunches of radishes, something which, in my youth, my grandmother had sliced into the salads she prepared for our family outings and which I'd removed and flicked into the grass beyond the picnic blanket. In the spring the cheese stand will set up between the tables of a woman who sells homemade dog treats and an oysterman from Matunuck. The girl in the red coat will not return. Neither will I see Cara again. In the spring I will not go to the market alone. Sharing the back seat of the car with their dog, I will go only when my friend and his wife do. I'll buy the dog a treat as a gesture of gratitude for my friend's indulging my persistent, though warrantless, paranoia about being alone should I encounter Cara. I'll also do it because I'm amused when, every time, the dog hesitates and acts as if its certain that I won't really relinquish the goodie before snatching it from my palm. When my friend picks me up from the airport, a little later in the spring, he'll apologize for having brought the dog with him on such a somber errand. It won't matter to me. In fact, I'll laugh just as readily when the dog looks at me expecting the treat I don't have as I do when the dog seems to think I might keep an offered treat for myself. The laughter will sound the same, but the feeling unfurling with it will be unfamiliar. In the spring the lie that had gone unspoken to Cara, the lie that I'd sown within myself, will at last bear its true fruit.

Roger Williams Park
Michael Crowley

There used to be more rest areas.
Now just the edge with litter
All over like mislead jonquils.
Too much in the sun those elms,
That oak left to poke around
For signs of cohabitation
Later wonder who where was
That rest area?

Park Rules
- Keep off the grass
- Curb your desires
- No unsanctioned abstractions
- Or opened pit fires

The Rose Garden
It looks like roses everywhere
Blooming a bright lipstick red,
And whites, yellowed with days.
Yellowpinks, salmonpinks
Framed in a green boxwood hedge
Then a garden path,
A trellis, whatever else you want:
Bees, trees in a breeze but not people.
You can't imagine people on this precipice.

Park Rules
- No walking, fast talking
- Casual encounters with puppets and clowns
- No dead, No mention of old lovers
- or getting upset over the least little

Photos
A girl in a green blouse
Another in a yellow slicker
Rained on interminably.
One's of a man in gray flannel
Like an ad-man with a boy in a sweatshirt,
Kurt Cobain on the front.
Another one of a girl, sleeveless
And a man not wearing socks
Like in brave new world.
These were all taken at the rose garden.

They're all black and white
People say it's not
All black or white but these are
Though the roses are colored.

Leaves
In a breeze, a red maple leaf,
The first to turn against me,
Chevrolets are everywhere without
Drivers like songs without singers.
All strangers, some without ties,
Others tied or tired, and now the fandango.
I turn to make sure no one is sneaking up
On the wrought iron bridge
With another side to the story.
A Weed Wacker Wails,
And some give up too soon

The Swans
With both hands
I push sunrise up
While the swans complain bitterly,
"We are not ducks to be toyed with,
We disdain your yolk
The onus of your line drawn
Your sticks and stones
And all the repetitiveness."

Park Rules
- No accusatory tones, off hand remarks,
- allusions to "other parks"
- Absolutely no suicidal soliloquies
- subtle innuendo
- No apocalypse now or later.

Julie Danho

Playing Hide and Seek in the Garden of Heroes
Providence, RI

I've never seen it before, this horseshoe of bushes
tucked at the front of the State House lawn,
like a pocket on a wide green shirt. It must be

a secret garden, I say to my daughter, so of course
she races over, and by the time I see those
short flags in the dirt, she's climbing up

the granite marker, pink sneakers muddying
the names of the dead. I pull her off, her limbs
flailing like a beetle on its back. *You only*

look, I say, and she shrugs, running fingers over
the engraving. She is three. Some of these soldiers
were alive when she was born. There is room left

for more. *Come find me*, she says, wedging
herself between the marker and the azaleas,
her feet and banged-up knees sticking out

over the gravel path. She is a terrible hider.
I sit on a wooden bench and count backwards
from ten, my eyes open. The slender redbuds

offer no cover, their crowns suited only
for ornament. It feels wrong to play here,
where people in uniform have mourned.

Some might believe the dead are happy
to see a child keep this garden alive,
but I look over my shoulder for a mother

or father who might see us and remember
playing until everyone was hot and tired.
I pretend not to find her, calling her name

until she laughs and shrieks, runs out
to grab me. I brought her here. For her,
I will hide and hope that no one sees.

Nancy Jasper

Amalia In Fox Point
~for Amalia Rodrigues

Yes, Amalia
visited Fox Point.
She muted her charisma.
She took a walk
in this small neighborhood,
not too far from the water.
She went to Friends Market.
It was stocked
with everything she remembered.
She paused for a picture
with the owner and his wife.
Even now,
she's not that far from us.
This morning,
on Ives Street,
Joe cues up
Amalia
on Pandora.
The fadista,
that veteran of distances,
slips into the room.

Favas
We share a bowl of fava beans
at the Holy Rosary feast.
On this summer night,
a parking lot becomes a plaza,
hung with lights.
Across the way,
the once a year Ferris Wheel
turns.
The large beans
do not resist the change.
Trading integrity for experience,
they are beginning to slip from their skins.

A Malasada Is Not A Doughboy

In the church garage,
the women are assembling
flour, sugar, eggs, and tricks
their grandmas knew.
Malasadas today,
after the Mass.
I want to get them bem quente,
right from the oil.
The sign on the garage reads:
Malasadas/Doughboys.
A malasada is not a doughboy.
Malasadas
have melismatic
turnings of flavor.
They don't give everything away
at the first bite.
Taste: the pleasure
will glide away from you a little,
like Portuguese vowels, like a word sung
by Amalia.
Dedicated to the malasadas
at the Holy Rosary Church in Fox Point.

Transit Street
In 1769,
citizen astronomers
built a platform
near streets now called Transit and Planet.
They assembled their instruments
to time
the Transit of Venus
as she passed
between Fox Point and the sun.
Today, a brass band
moves through this neighborhood.
The Holy Rosary
Pentecost procession.
The men's red ties
are memories of flames.
Banners, trumpets, drums,
the old desire
for a local connection to immensity

Holy Rosary Church [11]

TRI-X Providence
Susan Tacent

1. What's Missing?

What is it about doorways?
It is the liminal that attracts, the threshold, with its doubled promise of access and escape?

Or the doors themselves, the way they ride on hinges and respond to our touch?

We expect that doors lead somewhere. We expect that by passing through doorways we have accomplished something. We arrive at or depart from a dinner party, a hotel, the home of a beloved friend or family member, the workplace, our own quietly familiar room. Through doors we enter or leave museums, theaters, the supermarket. Cars, buses, and taxis have doors, as do trains and airplanes. Refrigerators have doors.

I took this photo years ago in Providence, Rhode Island, on Olney, I think, just past Prospect. It was the first time I lived in a new state. My zip code went from 10018 to 02906. The building in the photo loomed before me and I was attracted by the quirky absurdity of its three doors' placement relative to one another and the street. But I was saddened, too, struck by what seemed to be missing, and what felt like the silence of inaccessibility.

Doors are part of our emotional makeup. We can slam them shut, or holding our breath close them oh so softly. We can lock doors or leave them open.

2. Strings Attached

I grew up in Brooklyn. But for a few years, before I moved to Providence, I lived in Manhattan. My small apartment was on 36th Street between Fifth and Sixth, in a four story walk-up tucked like a forgotten child between two much larger buildings. On the ground floor, there was a very busy deli with its own entrance. I don't recall ever going in there though I must have.

The closer I came to leaving the city for Providence the fonder I became of it. I went alone to events, as if practicing for the day when everything around me would be unfamiliar. I remember walking the few blocks to the Macy's July Fourth Fireworks display, lavishly staged on the East River. In pre-9/11 New York, viewers were free to go as near as we wanted. Cracks of sound banged against buildings on both sides of the narrower streets. At the river's edge, light and color exploded overhead, like Close Encounters of the Third Kind come true.

I went to museums, libraries, the theater, as often as possible. I was like a rabid tourist, frothy in my need for overstimulation.

In AAAH OUI GENTY!, there was a puppet, described by John Corry (whose NY Times review I liked enough to clip inside the showbill) as "A Pierrot who looks uncomfortably like an unborn child, despite his floppy clown's clothing..." The puppet realizes it is strung at the shoulders, neck, and wrists. Corry writes how the puppet "stares mournfully at the puppeteer. He is mournful because he is being manipulated," Corry writes, "which tells us something about the nature of despondency." The puppeteer, I remember, was way at the top of the stage, where long, dark curtains dropped from a height of at least fifteen feet, covering the entire back of the stage. The puppet, to see who was holding the strings, had to crane his head back and up.

I remember this part of the show slowing down as the puppet came to his realization and then made a decision, but I can't say that memory is true. I know the section concluded with the puppet cutting all the strings and collapsing to the floor. I don't remember if there was music. I don't remember if the people around me, all strangers, cried out. I hope they did, and I with them.

3. Four Other Susans

Names are funny. We don them like armor, like perfume. Composed of abstract sequences of letters, still they delineate us. There were four other Susans in fifth grade. In our written work, we had to use the initial of our last names to differentiate ourselves.

The photo was taken in Fox Point, the neighborhood where I lived for a number of years as a graduate student. Even as I settled into my new life, photography quickly became a respite from the literary texts and heady, elusive, analysis I was being trained in. I scrounged extra cash for Kodak's TRI-X 400 black-and-white film, one 10-pack brick at a time, that I kept in my freezer. I developed the film myself after getting permission from the landlord to set up a makeshift darkroom in the back hallway of the first floor apartment I rented.

Upstairs lived three grad students from Greece, all physicists, all men. The building had two entrances. One day the physicists decided they wanted to use as their main entrance the one that housed my darkroom. I appealed to the landlord; he refused to take sides. Eventually the physicists and I reached a compromise.

Looking back, I am embarrassed and amazed, too, by how adamantly I insisted my need for a clean, dark space was greater than their need to throw nice parties. I wanted to be alone; they were hoping to put an end to loneliness.

4. School Paper

Mr. Levy was a white man in his early thirties. I recall very dark curly hair, thick glasses, a white button-down shirt, a plain tie, and deep blue trousers. He dressed the same way every day, I think. But that might be a trick of memory's wanting everything to be easier than it was. Mr. Levy was my seventh grade English teacher. He was also in charge of the school paper, an oversized print monthly with articles about fashion, poetry, school news, and sometimes, interviews. Some of my friends and I were editors and writers for the paper. One day, there was the opportunity for a few of us to go to Manhattan to interview a relatively new, up-and-coming film director. The morning of the trip, I got cold feet. I don't recall why. All I know is I told my mother I had a stomach ache and she let me stay home. Someone else got to do the interview. Even though he occasionally shoots films in Providence, no photo exists, at least not yet, of Woody Allen and me.

5. The Egg-like Object is a Stone

By the time I moved out of New York, I'd lived on my own or with friends in twelve different apartments and one house. I lived in my first apartment only for two weeks; the Italian landlady got one look at my black friends and politely but firmly told me she'd changed her mind about the lease. After New York, another seven different living arrangements. I'm an expert at packing; I know how disruptive and annoying the process of moving is.

Yet I still get a thrill looking at pictures of apartments for rent or houses for sale online. I can still trick myself into falling asleep by imagining furnishing an empty apartment, usually one I know well. Lately, I have been trying to remember a recurrent dream about houses that have extra rooms in them, rooms I'd forgot were there. Occasionally in these dreams I am touring other people through them- a metaphor for writing? The extra rooms generally are lush, neat, and all in a row on either side of a spacious corridor. The main feature is the extra space: there are places as yet unexplored. I always wake up from these dreams feeling happy and hopeful. The funny thing to me now is that in trying to recall them, I got fixated on which house or apartment it was that had inspired the dreams in the first place. I'm not even sure there was one place in particular.

Nostalgia literally means the pain of the journey home. For me, it's the excitement of discovering the place I dwell in is larger than I thought.

The photo was taken in the backyard of that Williams Street house I rented with two other roommates in Providence. It was the first time I lived in a house. I lived there for three years. I wrote my dissertation there. I read very old stories, late into the night. Family visited from New York and I toured them around Providence like a native. As time passed, I came to love that house, for its wide plank floors, high ceilings, ill-fitting windows, and generous spirit. The egg- like object in the photo is a stone.

6. Transit

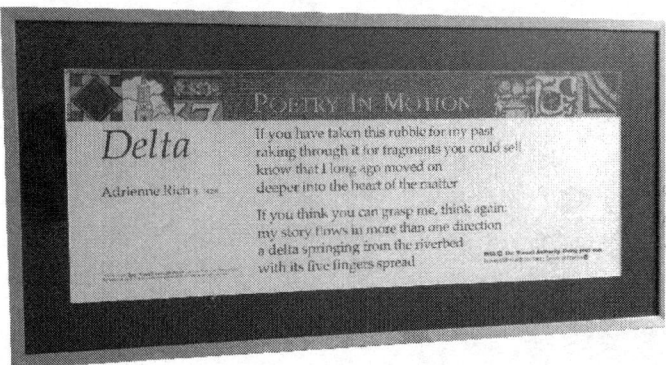

My sister and I rode the New York City subway system regularly when we were growing up. Our mother took decades' worth of rides on the L from Brooklyn to Manhattan and back. She was a secretary, and worked for a real estate company, lawyers, an investment firm. She wore makeup, had her hair done, and dressed in attire one might now wear to a fancy cocktail party or a wedding. We infrequently went with her to work. Or we took the trains to the beach. Or to a play, or museum, or shopping at one of the many department stores in downtown Brooklyn or the city.

As an adult, I took the D train to visit grandparents in Flatbush and Coney Island. The 6 got me to Hunter College. Often, during rush hour, I elbowed myself through the crowded platform and onto an overstuffed car so as not to be late for a class.

I never got motion sick on trains the way I did on buses and cars. The rocking lull, the roaring song, the subterranean trip. The sudden shrieking lurch to a stop, or creaky acceleration. The subway was as good as a best friend, the kind who's always willing to hold hands.

Sometimes it was difficult to stay awake. On how many rides did I sleep the sleep of the dead, while sharpening the twin skills of not falling out of the seat or missing my stop? For awake time there was an endless supply of reading material. There was the sidewise glance, aimed at the newspaper, magazine, or best seller of the person in the adjacent seat. There were the ads running the length of either side of every car. The photo is of a piece of framed subway art, from the time when art on the trains was a thing and my sister knew someone who knew someone.

When we were little, our mother told us if either of us ever got separated from her on the train, we should get off at the next stop and wait there. She would come back and find us. I don't know why, but I was never scared that would happen, and it never did. I wish I could remember the first time I rode the subway by myself. It must really have been something.

Underground travel is like having access to a giant secret; yes, shared with a bunch of other people, but that only makes it better. It took me a while to accept the fact that there was no subway in Providence. At Andreas, a restaurant on Thayer Street, I pretended the rumble of the bus going by was a train, passing determinedly beneath me while I ate.

7. Pray for Me

Soeur Caritas and I became friends one summer at an academic program in literature. As a non- practicing Jew, I didn't know quite what to make of her. Soeur Caritas was in France on a scholarship. She was from Burundi. Her country was dangerous, she told me. She had been jailed there several times for political reasons.

One night, we were strolling Avignon's balmy, crowded streets and a homeless man caught at her robe and told her he was suffering. He asked her to pray for him. He spoke slowly, his French easy to understand. She told him he didn't need her prayers; she asked him to pray for her. After we moved on, I told her her answer had surprised me. She said she believed the man would help himself more if he stopped thinking of himself and offered her help instead.

There were times it was difficult for me to be in France. It felt very far from home, and home, for the first time, seemed not to be in Brooklyn, where I grew up and most of my family lived, or Manhattan, but Providence.

I left Avignon a few weeks earlier than Soeur Caritas. She'd admired my oversized tote bag, and I left it with her. I also had a device I'd purchased there to kill the mosquitoes that swarmed our rooms. It looked like a night light and plugged into the wall socket. It came with pink paper inserts that stank of chemicals. The mosquitoes were tiny, but loud and insistent; they buzzed your ears all night, making it impossible to sleep. I used the device sparingly, weighing sleep against the inhalation of toxins. I asked Soeur Caritas whether she wanted it and she did. She gave me her photo. We exchanged addresses. We stayed in touch via mail until I didn't hear from her.

8. Stop Looking

My sister and I weren't supposed to feed the kittens, but we did. They were offspring of strays. They annoyed the landlord, who acted friendly, and wasn't. We found homes for all three. I'm still in Rhode Island, and, though I live just outside Providence now, I'm in the small city almost every day. It's where I drink coffee, browse bookstores, buy freshly baked bread, go to the museum, see a movie, meet friends. Even before I moved to Providence, I was looking for a home for myself, a place where staying took up more of my attention than leaving. I can stop now.

In a Blizzard
James Crews

The night was alive with falling snow—
white hiding the dome of the Capitol
until, from a distance, it looked like
one of those cairns the Inuit used to stack
at each pass, a heap of stones in the shape
of a man they could stop and talk to,
or reach out and touch with stiff hands
when the mountain wind cut too close.
As I rounded the frozen river, I saw it
on the fresh snow—a cigarette, not yet wet
or ruined. And though I'd quit years ago,
I picked it up, slipped it in my pocket
and ducked into a diner where I begged
matches and a cup of steaming coffee.
Almost home, I held that hot Styrofoam
up to the plow now grinding along my street,
toasting the unseen man spreading rocksalt
like alms, lending some noise to the rows
of tucked-in houses his yellow lights
kept caressing. I stepped onto my porch,
struck a match and lit the cigarette,
letting the smoke bloom in the bitter air
where it hovered for an instant
as if it couldn't bear to leave me.

Missing Providence

Capitol, Providence, RI [13]

PART III

DEPARTURE

Missing Providence

Aaron Samuels

Born – 1992
after Jeanann Verlee

I was born of Edgewood, born of Al-Mall quickie mart
slash hookah bar slash pizza parlor slash ministry, born
of South Providence next door, with their chimi trucks
and speed bumps, called us *edge-hood*, called us *E-dubb*
called us secret handshakes, secret language, from *fachii*,
and *boss-man, bogue-rocks*—mom couldn't understand
a damn word—born of Warwick next door, their strip malls
and baseball and long roads, born of Broad Street, Park Ave,
bicycles with pegs to stand on and handle bars to sit—
three to a bike: *no problem*; born between exurb
and ghetto flanks, the water pulling us together
beneath our city, its soft hands, born of Narragansett Bay,
of low tide, of white geese

covered in black oil.

Born – Summer 1996
after Jeanann Verlee

In first grade summer camp
the counselors pelican-marched us
to the bamboo & sludge
of the Narragansett Bay,
told us to pick up sea glass.
My mother said
they made a bunch of six-year-olds pick up glass?
We came home with jars full,
softened colored shards,
remnants of broken bottles
left in the salt water.
I kept as much as I could under my bed,
took some out each sundown, ran my fingers
along the edges, tipped my salted tongue
to the top part of the ocean,
pretended to crunch—
take that glass away from your face!
My mother lifted me up by my neck skin,
looked at all of the places I could bleed from,
watched me run barefoot
down the middle of the road
back to an ocean filled with glass.

She called it love, but really
it was a warped and seasoned fear:
that any broken thing would break
again.

Born – Broad Street, Winter 2001
after Jeanann Verlee

I was not born   in   Edgewood   no one is born
in Edgewood   but we move and settle
until the water and salt hardens us   scabbed fist in my pocket
bag of peas in my freezer   born of Edgewood   where
the hardest out was the boy who could take the most punches
still smile sea salt the next day   born of America   Online CDs
in bulk stolen from Wal-Mart   and garage doors
to tape them to   bb guns to shoot them with

born of pornography   Kevin's divorced father left it in the
VCR   we made fun of the first one to get a boner   and the
last   it was unanimously agreed that it was cool   because
everyone had their own blanket   it was definitely not gay

born of the poker game on Friday night in the basement of
Kevin's house   Kevin had bought a bike from a boy
named Jimmy behind Luchetti's restaurant while I
kept look out   when the poker game gossip told us Jimmi had
sold us a stolen bike   we pelican-marched to the other side of
town   took the money   back Edgewood style,
we kept the bike, smoked *bogue-rocks* in our triumph
boss-man

I won poker that winter night   called *fachii*   walked home
with a pocket full of seventy five dollars   my dick folded up behind
my belt loop   ears tucked into a fitted cap
a silver Star of David salting my neck   shining in the midnight
like stained glass

Sens Francois, English Misleading
Alyssa Copeland

I should practice my French more often
so I can tell complete strangers,
"Je suis solitaire."
They'll think I'm a lost tourist
and give me directions in English
to the Biltmore or the Providence Place Mall
or they'll think I'm a well-dressed crazy off the street
and give me change
in exchange
for silence.

I often see myself as an American Amelie,
using my imagination
to fill in the lonely gaps
while I use language
to tell them in English,
"No, I'm sorry. I'm fine."

When I study French,
I get lost in the gender differences
entre la lettre et le journal -
the way that you have to close your eyes
to catch the subtle nuances of
plurals vs. singulars.
It helps me accept that,
when it comes to my personal life,
no matter the gender, it makes no difference,
I still miss the subtle nuances -
even when counted among plurals,
I find myself singular.

To help assuage my vernacular isolation,
I think of the apartment for rent above Avery Piano.
Every time I walk past,
beautiful visions fill my head the rest of the day -
writing poetry on the balcony
to the sound of practice and the echoes of crowds;
my cat purring softly in the cup of my hand
so I can drink in her whispers
when it grows just too quiet.
I'd send postcards to my moms, sans the gnomes,
knowing it's not enough to make her stop missing me.

I'd take a cup of tea every evening,
settling in with the dusk of the day,
counting the colored shadows walking down below
on the streets of a city I'm too scared to embrace,
so I let the darkness tuck me in.

Sera les clous dans mon cercueil.

Hassan St. [14]

The Expiration Date
Avelino de Castro

On the day Martin Graves was supposed to die, he didn't. The day came and went, and he didn't die.

The date was September 21, 2243. Medical science had advanced to such a degree that the exact time and cause of death, barring accidents, could be determined at birth. When babies were born, their date of death was branded on the heel of their right foot.

When Martin got out of bed on September 22nd, smiling sheepishly, his wife Kat snorted, "Stubborn. You were always so stubborn."

The night before she had prepared a dinner for him that included all his favorite foods: lasagna, pot roast, Italian Easter pie, and Champagne.

On his last night his two children, Katarina and Mary, and their husbands Joe and Fred visited. His two grandchildren, Joe Jr., and Mary Anne sat on his lap one last time.

In his bedroom Martin set his patent leather shoes, well polished that morning with Kiwi shoe polish, under the bed, folded up his clothes for Goodwill, and went to bed that night, ready for the massive stroke that would kill him.

The stroke never came. He woke up on the morning of the 22nd and greeted the day with delight. The sound of the birds chirping and tweeting outside was almost unbearably beautiful.

His wife Kat was angry with him. "What are you trying to do Martin? You've lived a hundred forty years. You worked for eighty years. We had a great retirement. What are you trying to pull?"

"Maybe it's just not my time yet?"

"Your time is stamped right there, on your right foot. If you don't die tonight, and die properly, I'm going to take action."

"What are you going to do, kill me?"

"Of course not, I'm going to call a lawyer. I think you should go to the doctor in the meantime, find out just what's going on."

Martin Graves took his wife's advice and visited his family physician, Dr. Chang. The Doctor fit Martin in his busy schedule at ten a.m. From eight to nine-thirty Martin hung around the duck pond, at the park, feeding the ducks.

Dr. Chang tested Martin thoroughly, then said, "I don't know what to make of it Martin. You should have died last night, but your brain scan shows nothing. There's no plaque in your brain to cause the stroke. You will die eventually, but the system's not perfect. I suggest you just enjoy the extra time."

Martin shrugged his shoulders, and went home. Kat was waiting for him. "What did Dr. Chang say?"

'He said the system's not perfect, and my brain is fine."

"Well that's it then. You can just get out, and talk to my lawyer."

Martin was hurt, but he realized that his wife's expiration date was in 2265. Obviously she had plans for the rest of her time that didn't include him.

Martin called his daughter Katarina, and asked, "Can I stay with you for awhile? I should be dead any day now. It's just a fluke that I'm still alive."

Katarina resisted, "We really don't have any place to put you. You'd have to sleep on the couch. And I don't know what we'd tell Joe Jr. He thinks you're already dead."

Martin sighed, "I can always ask Mary."

Katarina probed, "Mom won't let you stay with her?"

"She's pretty adamant that I get out right away."

Katarina relented, "Well just come on over. You can stay here. But don't fight it. You're supposed to expire on your expiration date."

Martin sighed, "I know."

Kat had filled two suitcases with clothes for Martin, and left them by the front door. She handed him a sheet of paper. She mumbled, "That's my lawyer's information." Then she shouted, "Now just go die, already!"

Martin took the monorail to Cranston. Then he caught a hover cab, and rode to Katarina's house, 414 Main Road. He paid the driver three hundred forty dollars and gave him twenty for a tip.

He was down to two thousand, six hundred, forty-two dollars.

He stood on the front step of Katarina and Joe's colonial house with his battered suitcases, and heard loud raised voices inside.

Joe shouted, "He was supposed to die yesterday. What's he trying to pull?"

Katarina defended her father, "I hardly think he's stayed alive on purpose. He knows how much of an imposition he is."

Joe raged, "He's going to have to sleep on the couch. I'm not going to bed early for him. Christ. Do you think he'll die tonight?"

Katarina howled, "I don't know! How can I know these things? My mother called. She said he went to the doctor, and the doctor said he was fine. But that doesn't mean he couldn't have a stroke tonight."

"I just hope he catches up. Maybe his expiration date was just off by a day. Jesus, I really don't want his body stinking up our house."

"You're talking about my father."

Martin took that as a sign to knock on the door.

He heard Katarina hiss, "He's here."

Joe opened the front door, and scowled at Martin, "Well, you'd better come in if you're staying."

Martin asked, "Where's Joe Jr.?"

Katarina kissed Martin on the cheek, a cold kiss. She said, "He's staying with Mary until, you know, we didn't want him to get more attached to you. You should be expiring any day now."

Katarina made a fine dinner for them. Roast chicken with roasted red bliss potatoes and asparagus.

Martin sat on the sofa, slowly falling asleep, while Joe watched the evening programs he liked on the television.

Katarina made up the couch with sheets and pillows, and kissed her father on the forehead. As she headed for the stairs, she said to her father, "Goodbye."

But Martin didn't go anywhere. He woke early. He felt fine, and healthy.

The three of them ate breakfast.

The young folks went to work, and Martin went to the bank to get some money.

The teller said, "My computer lists you as deceased."

"But I'm very much alive. You can surely see that."

The teller smiled wanly. "Not according to my records."

Martin went to the park and fed the ducks.

He received a text message on his iPhone. It was from the law firm of Schlick, Miester and Schlick. It read, "This is an official notice of annulment from Kat Graves to Martin Graves. Martin Graves, legally declared dead, despite any evidence to the contrary, cannot hold Kat Graves to a binding legal contract of marriage. This marriage is annulled due to the fact that Martin Graves has been legally declared dead by an act of the Third District Court of Providence County. The presiding judge in the case is Georgiana Fossbender."

Martin sighed, and walked to the monorail. He was dejected. They could just declare you dead, just like that without you even being there to prove them wrong. He rode back to Cranston, and walked back to Katarina's house.

His daughter and son-in-law were still at work. He studied his shoes. When he was a boy he had shined shoes for money on the street in Providence. He remembered those days as some of the best of his life. He looked down at his well polished shoes and cried quietly.

Around five, Joe came home from his construction job to find Martin sitting on the front step. He scowled, "You still alive?"

Martin shrugged his shoulders, "I can't help it."

Joe let Martin into the house, and gave him a beer. They sat in front of the TV for a couple of hours until Katarina came home from Miriam hospital and her nursing job. She ordered pizza from a local pizzeria that delivered, and they ate pizza and drank soda for dinner. She barely looked at Martin, and didn't speak to him at all. After dinner she said, "Goodbye dad," as though that might ensure that he finally die in his sleep, and she climbed the stairs to her bedroom.

Joe lingered on the couch, watching TV until well after Martin fell asleep, slouching on the couch. Nobody brought him sheets or pillows.

He woke up at four in the morning. He decided to leave the house. He wandered to the monorail station and went into Providence. When the stores opened, he got himself a shoe shine kit for twenty-five hundred dollars. He went down to Kennedy Plaza, and set up his shoeshine gear on the stone steps near the young boys that were shining shoes. He shined shoes all day, and finally felt good. He didn't know how much longer he was going to live, or where he was going to sleep, but he was a good shoe shine man, and that was all that mattered.

Robin Dionne

Like Christmas
Late last spring you found me,
secretly watching from above
while I searched
all twenty-seven thousand square feet
for you.
Over half of a year,
we became sad songs
and long drives,
coffee and
new lines on my skin.
This winter,
I will
keep collecting
the small things,
writing them down until morning,
happy for now,
because we are
sleepless for the same reason.

The Names You Will Not Call Me
Three years ago, you made a deal
with a different smiling woman
but now,
driving home,
it is my voice
you are looking for.
I have always struggled to be
committed without committing,
practicing on unsuspecting others,
and
I am paying for it now,
these ten thousand tiny love notes
as currency that
I cannot exchange
for
the things that I want.

Letting My Hair Grow
I have spent the year
following cigarettes and sawdust,
solving for unknown variables
at the end of the alphabet
and
when I said that your love
is always a day too early,
what I really meant is
I have learned
to set my watch.

Time and Materials
It is the coldest night of the year
and I am working late,
checking the locks
and taking your pulse,
trading my short stories
to you and the ghosts
in exchange for
whiskey and the wrong words,
waiting to connect the dots
or draw the line between them.

**The Exterior of the Building Next Door
and What it Felt Like to Finish the Job**
In the same corner
at the same bar
last night
in the little city,
I explained the meniscus,
– the tension on the surface of our drinks
and you said
"besides my grandmother's watch
what else do you have up your sleeve?"

City Hall, Providence, RI [15]

Providence
Antonia Farzan

The first time that I saw Narragansett Beer for sale outside Rhode Island was at Littleneck, a bar located down the street from the South Brooklyn Casket Company. It's designed to look like an ironic version of the clam shacks that featured prominently in my Rhode Island childhood, where you are given a shell painted with your order number and sent to wait at the picnic tables by the sandy parking lot, and where seagulls methodically eat their way through abandoned plates of French fries. I assumed that serving Gansett was a part of the joke.

After that, though, I started seeing it everywhere I went in Brooklyn, generally selling for $5 a can. Some bar menus earnestly listed "Providence, Rhode Island" as the source, not realizing that it was actually brewed in Rochester. A few of my friends, completely missing the point, asked me if it was any good. It had replaced PBR, I was told by bartenders, as the cheap beer of choice for the sort of urban hipsters who made PBR a cliché in the first place.

I should have been enthusiastic about this development. Narragansett's comeback has been one of the few unquestionable successes of post-industrial Providence. (Regardless of where it's made, the company is run by a Rhode Islander and headquartered on Ship Street.) And being associated with inexpensive beer is arguably better than the other choices: high unemployment, ubiquitous Dunkin' Donuts franchises, corruption, and the short boring stretch of Interstate 95 that passes through Coventry.

But that Rhode Island—the Rhode Island of snowplow kickback schemes and burnt-tasting coffee—is the Rhode Island that I love, in a perverse sort of way. Tourists come for clam shacks and seaside B&Bs, but when I think about home, it's the Providence shoreline, with its scrap metal, smokestacks, and strip clubs, that I find myself missing. The kind of place where Gansett was once consumed unironically, by fishermen before the industry collapsed and by factory workers before their jobs went overseas.

The fact that I feel this way has more to do with possessiveness than anything else. Like any Rhode Islander, I'm used to handing over the best parts of the state to people from Massachusetts, Connecticut, and New York. But the stretch of Allens Avenue along the Providence River? That's safely ours. There's no charm in oil terminals and highway ramps, and that's why I love it: because no one else seems to.

My resistance to people drinking Narragansett in Bushwick studios and Gowanus bars came from the same weirdly protective impulse, I eventually realized. As irrational as it sounds, seeing those red-and-white retro-styled cans in the hands of people who couldn't pick out Cranston on a map made me feel like they were taking away something that was supposed to belong to us.

People in New York often accuse Providence of being a "shitty city," especially if they went to Brown or RISD. While I disagree with them, I'm careful not to argue too much. There's no imminent danger of Providence becoming "the next Brooklyn," but I worry about what will happen if too many people discover everything that makes it strange and wonderful. I might be ambivalent about Rhode Island—I moved away, after all—but that doesn't mean that I'm ready to hand it over.

I don't want to see people wearing vintage Free Buddy t-shirts or describing this great new spot in Olneyville unless they grew up here, spending Friday nights hanging out in front of the Store 24 on Thayer Street. And I don't want them drinking our beer, either. Not unless they know what it's like to constantly contemplate leaving for some place more proportionate with their ambition, while also knowing that no other city will belong to them in quite the same way.

It doesn't matter what I think, though. Last weekend, I met up with some friends in Greenpoint. All the bars there have started serving Genesee Light.

Shall Providence progress from these

to bare cleanliness

or to gardens?

The Houses of Providence [16]

Wynton Marsalis at the VMA
David O'Connell

I heard and your mother heard the music, though I was on the aisle
and she was wedged between my knee and the handbag of the woman
with a butterscotch. "I've got a butterscotch,"
she was whispering to the man with the cough, which is to say
my concentration and your mother's, by her own admission,
wasn't only on the music, which was familiar, the way a face
on TV once was (bomb scare—cop show—and the paramedic
in the background a girl I once mooned over). I was so grateful then
for the legroom, my left foot keeping time in the aisle
as Marsalis, red mute at the bell of his trumpet, was waving goodbye
to his own pursed lips. Mood Indigo, I realized. We were away from you
for the first time. Providence lit for the holidays. All the way in,
our visible breath. Coffee, we decided. After. This was years ago
and when I think of it, the pitch of the second balcony
that kept me falling from my seat and over the rail each time
I shut my eyes to listen, the melody holds on. I could play it for you,
easily a hundred slightly varied versions. But your mother,
that handbag, the woman with a butterscotch, its golden cellophane
endlessly unwrapped, a sudden absence of her husband's
phlegmy hack, Marsalis at center stage, his hand fluttering the mute,
one note bleeding to the next—Elizabeth, I mean,
I was there. Both I and your mother. And then again the cold,
our breath, the coffee forgotten in the short ride back to you.

In Response to Sam Teitel's Letter to NY or, Let me tell you a story:
Astrid Drew

While Captain Kidd was allegedly
Marauding the high seas, Boston's governor
Rabidly pursued him via paper & courtrooms
Shunning New York as the birthplace
Of such a robber baron, a nest of evil
He scolded little Rhody
For supposedly sheltering those
Veterans of the swashbuckling trade
He demanded their release
Into Boston's hall of moral justice
For crimes they may, or may not, have committed.

New York ignored her cousin city
Laughed as she welcomed new ships
Into watery crevices
While RI's Governor Cranston
Essentially bestowed the middle finger
In Boston's general direction.
Whatever "Fuck You" was in 1690.
A curt dismissal from lives
He had no business in meddling.

That same Puritanical pretension lingers under cobblestones
I can smell it on your breath as you rave against your age-old rival

I know New York irks you, that behemoth city
Belching noise and money
But what you see as aloof arrogance
is actually hardship tattooed into stiff necks
Determination chewed in jaws like wormy tobacco
To live in a city that should have sunk
Into the swamp it sprang from ages ago.

Cause the truth is:
Dreams go to Boston to study and stagnate
In New York they leap suicidal from skyscrapers
They shatter or fly.
If New York is the bloated over-achieving sibling
Boston is the younger brother bitching about that shadow
And guess what? They're both fucking aggravating.

Missing Providence

Cause the truth is:
In 1690, Rhode Island was also called
Rogue's Island
an apt nickname for a place
founded by exiles
whose people spit revolution
years before gunpowder dregs
caught fire beneath Massachusetts lantern light
Where in a single night in dinky Warwick, RI
colonists, drunk and hasty
shot a British captain
and burned his frigate to the waterline.

You love your city and that's just fine
But don't pin accolades where they don't belong.
Personally, I prefer itty bitty Providence
Where buildings are short, but spirit runs long.
A city built by merchants and thieves
Whose corruption is apparently hereditary, but hey
My jewel in rough political muck & mire
There is something here that lives nowhere else
And I'm not talking about waterfire
But similar

A life that floats above the flood
haven for heretics and eccentrics

If dreams go elsewhere
To bloom or obliterate
They are born here
Within a den of rogues.
We say, take cues from Roger
Row against the current
And burn ships for ideas.

Funeral
Kik Williams

when he died
we were
given valiums
and alcohol

there were no tears
as I led
my younger
siblings
up the aisle

we followed
his casket
to the front
of the church

I wore
my first
black dress
with a jacket
to match
and a fall
of streaked
human hair
my father's
girlfriend
gave me
to cover
my dirty hair

I just
realized
this is my
mother's
funeral
nine months
later
not
my father's

she would
never let
me
wear
a black dress
at seventeen
and I would
have screamed
it should
have been
you

Necromancer
Meghan Friedmann

I am at my most raw. Sifting through reams of silk,
counting and uncounting the hours.
A pattern shocks me with forgotten beauty.
I hold the fabric to my face,
wash tired skin in ghost material,
weep as if water could weave;
parts fade like writing on a chalkboard
once purposeful and defined
now asking to be retraced
or put to death.

     The markings
can never be recaptured
in exactness
and the color, like emotion,
is even harder.

Sometimes I drown myself
don't come out for days
remain covered in elusive ripples
that others are afraid to touch.
Sometimes I wrap myself up
hoping tulle works like armor. It doesn't.
Forgetting all it needs to do
is brush me with a butter knife,
the atmosphere shoots arrows instead.
When one hits, I can't move my eyes
from the hole, the blood that obliterates
and replaces.

     Sometimes
the phone rings. Your voice
like a possibility.

False Starts (Kelsey)
Everett Epstein

1.
    You blacked out while reading my tarot, stumbling over the *Hanged Man* description; drunkenly pressing your fingertip into the laminate card, into the figure's inverted chest. Your prophecy slipped into that slurred 2 A.M. shibboleth. "...ok... so, this is not good... it's, in fact, terrible... just not good... for you, I mean... the hanged man... you know this..." In that moment, you tapped some subterranean well, ventriloquized the beyond. Perhaps because, as you trailed off, you communed with this ocean, traced the gnomic topography of oblivion's sea-floor. Reading the braille written by tides above. As your finger pressed further into the card, as your finger began to support your full weight, I could only guess the depths you'd plumb.

2.
    Eyes: two lustrous pupils, soapstone ovals, Delphic. Your face obscured by muddy bangs, charcoal gossamer. Us both squinting. I conjure you from memory, relying less on pictures — themselves difficult to find (you relied on Eliot's Facebook for gossip)— and more on the unevenly canted script scrawled across postcards, decorated with Mannerist paintings or national parks. You: a compilation, an assemblage, a constellation across Providence.

    The ash tray outside your Thayer apartment; the cupola surveying the hutch of tree branches; coffee-stain bruises from dead-arms; "Blow-Up," and Bora, and Travis, and Nick; your birthday cards; the Vermont cabin; the black tufts nested in your armpits when you put your hair up; a kitchen secreted in the dorm room basement; Kirk's mangled wisdom teeth — his caries pooling with blood as he descended the stairs.

3.
    Us slumped into the lecture halls seats of Salomon—I: prattling on about music, trying to trip some wire; you: cooly interrogating the Sun hovering over the stage, and I mentioned Okkervil River, and your enthusiasm bubbled to the surface.

4.
    You didn't realize how much your excitement meant to me. It served as both a culmination and an introduction; this was the last memory I have of music shouldering the weight of teenage significance. Of it imbued with meaning, artifice, communion. And in gesturing to the past, we inadvertently propelled ourselves towards a future, stumbling forwards. Encanted beneath the sun, these words conveyed us headlong into a new world that ironically tempered all magic — be it cabalistic spells or tarot. Yet, you remained that gateway.

Missing Providence

5.

2 A.M. October: I walked to your clapboard house, paint chips sloughing off in snakeskin reams, ascended the scoured concrete steps, and knocked against the glass framing the door. A light was on in the kitchen, and through the clouded glass, I saw you approach. As you came closer, your form focused, and I had the impression that soon you'd emerge, soon you surface. The door opened, and assuming a new aperture, the contours of your face sharpened.

6.

You applied black lipstick once and kissed the lower lefthand corner of your bathroom mirror, your pucker captured — a screen print on the glass. You never wiped it from that corner, even after you left that clapboard house; I can only assume the mark's perfect symmetry amused you, or at least, the tiny black heart complemented a life lived asymmetrically.

Did I make this up? Where was I in the room? Were you dressing for Travis's or Nika's? In the reflection, the mark just hovered, a snide bubon, a delinquent parade float right above my right cheek.

7.

You twined your paracord laces around your right index finger, pulling them tight, leaving a pink ring briefly tattooed around your digits. They eventually faded.

8.

Emily and I piled into Louis, the 5-to-5 diner, their chrome deco chairs stacked on the counters, the tables pushed to the side to make space for a makeshift stage. Every face embarrassingly recognizable, as is the case when you're 23 and living another year in the town where you went to school. Inevitably, by the time Nightmom played, I found you, dressed in coral organdy, leaning against the back wall, one army boot crooked behind the other. Nick screamed through minor chords, Travis plucking away at the Moog behind the drum kit, draping the stage in scuzz .

We spoke later, our voices hoarse from the joint choruses, our hearing cloaked by a gentle tinnitus chime. Our last spring together, the pavement swathed in shuttering damp. The sidewalk outside Louis bore teenage catechisms, haunted messages delivered from '03 and '94 and '86 to us. These concrete garbled cursives felt relevant to your exit from that scene, that show, and inevitably that town. Our town, once.

But all we said was "Travis has the best drummer face."

9.

Figure drawing class met on Wednesdays, secreted away in the 4th floor classroom of that brutalist brick topping Williams St. The usual model, a lithe 24 year old whose chest hair brilloed outwards in tiny strawberry-blonde cursives and whose clothes he buried in a Harrow Lacrosse bag, commanded the dais with obscene authority. Today, his doppelgänger, an older woman with ginger curls and razor sharp clavicles, bisected the stage with radial precision.

You constructed her body from disconnected shapes, balancing three ovids atop charcoal triangles. The skeletal drawing gesturing, commanding the gentle appliqué of a fingertip to smear together her body. To arrive at the reticulant whole.

10.
Here's a surefire way to make you laugh; you pull up "basset hound [or hounds] running in slow motion" on Youtube. Mute the sound and pause it. Then find the 1:11 sec "Jurassic Park Theme" in a separate window. Turn the volume way up, and press play on both videos.

This works well with the following pairings:
 A. "smiling sloth" +"Bruises"
 B. "badgers bbc" + "Feel the Lightning"
 C. "slow motion french bulldog" + The Raiders of the Lost Ark Theme

11.
The dawn split the floor boards into a geometry of taupe and dioxide orange. Split my face, dousing the left cheek in morning light. Contouring the craters of a spongey nostril, the furrowed operation of a forehead, hair diaphanous static.

5:45, blinking 16-bits. A digital carillon screaming out the alarm's laminate face, announcing each day's beginning like the Second Coming. Blinkered by the fog of dried tears, I clicked "Snooze," reacquainting the woken self for 10 minutes with the submerged dreamer. With the dream (reoccurring), wherein I refuse to acknowledge the tree recumbent in bed. The tree that bears 40 distinctive stone fruits, its roots fitful, ankled rictus. Bonita peaches and Tilton apricots rosacea amid the pluming plum flowers.

The tree is you. The grafted limbs calligraphed an obvious resemblance. Whispering in the A.C. of the one bedroom, the pliant tamarind shoots shudder; their amaranth buds nearly speaking, nearly offering an honest assessment of our 4 years, nearly completing my tarot reading, when the alarm starwipes your voice into digital fleece.

5:55 and the grain of the wood floor can be easily discerned: aspen. This was a big selling point on the Evergreen condo, which was distinctive from the one I just awoke. The dream-room wholly dun, whereas mine had one wall painted deep azure — applied in thick brushstrokes five weeks into the lease. According to *The Times*, this helped with sleep.

12.
Dave's Coffee. Loose dregs, slipped past the filter, peppering the surface. Buoyed along, the cream effloresced. I hurriedly supped from the crossword puzzle mug.

14-down: "Connective Maneuver."

Olneyville Graffiti Update
by Jacob Khepler for Mothers News
from Mothers News issue 39 April 2014

- The battle for the wall at AutoZone is pretty much over I guess--it was back and forth for a while between the people at AutoZone painting the wall grey and (probably) one person casually drawing a long lazy line across it. Maybe Lazy Line stopped walking around late at night? Maybe they work early in the morning now? Maybe they moved, or they're dating someone with Netflix or something, who knows?

- The old Rent-A-Center across from the Dunkin Donuts has a really nice feature right now that's just the center of the Wu Tang "W" design--if the W is a soaring eagle, this is the Brancusi version. Very nice!!! Also I walked by it on the sidewalk a hundred times without seeing it, then I saw it from across the street at the 7-11 and it was like looking up and seeing a cloud literally spell out your name. Did they plan on doing the wings last, but then a car came / door opened / goose honked / bear? Probably wise from both a design decision and a practical crime decision to do the intricate internal part first and then the expansive and expressive wings (NB). If tomorrow the wings are filled in I honestly don't know how I'll feel! With Brancusi's "Bird in Space", there is a feeling that the wings have become vestigial and dissolved--no atmosphere, no need. With this "infinite Wu" the design is similar but I feel that the opposite effect is achieved--the wings are vast, resolving at infinity. The wings include the old supermarket, the parking lot, all Manton Ave, all Providence, all world. It also appears as a candle and flame, illuminating all. In this schema, to draw the wings in would be to define the reach of the candle's glow. Anyway great piece, thanks to this person or this collection of situations (this car / door / goose / bear).

- Unfortunately the mural under the Rt 10 bridge over Westminster St is still untouched months after its construction. I understand that there's a general conduct among writers to let a piece fly for awhile, or maybe there's a fear of going over someone who's vindictive, but this is a legal wall--does this code still apply? Also it's depressing!!!!!! It's a bunch of CCTV cameras with kind human eyes hovering over the planet? Come on, that sucks. Graffiti can be commentary but a mural has to be inspirational, that's the law of murals (NB: Guernica is both, besides which Picasso paid his dues). I walk a block out of my way to avoid it, same feeling as a bank of real cameras. Ay, check this out: satire sucks (in 2014). To hell with NSA going Pokemon on personal data and to hell with this cheery oppressive (or nothing riff) legal wall in legacy anti-oppression format.

- MEGA DITTOS to the Shepard Fairey mural behind AS220!!!! God, why is this still burning???? I recognize dude's ties to town, but this is Kmart shit (or to be precise, Urban Outfitters). No one in this town has a fire extinguisher full of paint? Corny, useless, lazy, ugly, need I go on? OBEY is an eternally shitty message/brand- no recoup. They Live still a great movie tho.

- The other Rt 10 bridge, over Broadway, is looking pretty gnarly right now, but still feels good and fun in the original desired way. Get some good looks at it before someone paints a loft apartment on it--it's a classic "children live here / we are the future / ecology / multi cultural" mural. I love this mural mode, It's second only to Huge Whale Mode. Shout out to that animal protection mural in Somerville MA where a ring of people stand vigilant around a green earth full of animals and the representative people of the earth include Frederick Douglas, Mark Twain, and Elvira. That's a mural! Shout out to that one guy who spent the 80s painting massive whales over ugly corporate bullshit. That's a life.

- PEACE to Shane Jones for putting up cool confusing flyers on the street then UPDATING THEM! Great feeling, good mood, very messy, with crayon. Does a kid help? Street art qua "street art" absolutely sucks, but full marks to a weird nut taping shit to a light post because "here's what I'm doing tonight". To you, the reader--if a child gives you a cool drawing, don't put it on the fridge, tape it to a lamppost. Use a lot of tape. Also,,, is this a pseudonym? Seems crazy as a pseudonym but it also seems crazy to to write your given name extremely legibly on lampposts up and down the street.... I almost feel guilty writing it in a newspaper.... Ah, what do I know? (nothing)

- GYER still doing great work--they caught a bunch of nice tags over the summer, written in expanding foam. This really grossed out Kate Schapira, who thought it was mustard and got doubly, even triply grossed out when I touched the tag to determine its composition. I don't like to upset Kate Schapira but at the same time I do a little bit, because we're friends, that's why I do it for some reason.

- RIP to POW, that's sad, he got hit by a car while walking on the highway. Be careful out there everyone, I watched with bemusement last year as his tags in the parking lot got vigilante buffed by someone with a big messy can of pink paint. "WHAT'S YOUR NAME" was his angry response (in paint, same wall), but to no avail, he was playing chess (or checkers anyway) with a shadow. He passed away chasing (presumably) a different shadow, RIP. He seemed like a nice guy, I had a pleasant talk with him once, RIP. Be careful out there everyone!

Missing Providence

- Favorite long-running tag is whoever wrote EROS behind the Walgreens on Reservoir Ave. I know I mentioned this before but I just want to say it again. It's the little things in life, you know. To me, this is a feeling akin to a cat saying, "Hello". I like it with the awareness that with repetition this will leap into very obnoxious. But right now, this once, behind the Walgreens, "Hello."

- Most sincere head-scratcher is whoever's been writing LOFT all around the new Olneyville Square bullshit developments. No idea how to take this--is it commentary, sales tactic, or "just a word you like" (traditional)? Also, what will happen to the old Olneyville Obscure Entertainment Complex, now being developed? Will it be Renters Who Complain or Nothing For An Extremely Long Time? It's a tough call, and difficult to imagine any other options, but I would bet choice B. After all Brian Chippendale is 2 for 2 in getting evicted from a place that is speculated into nothingness--this future implied nothingness would give him the hat trick. But uhhhhh prove me wrong, America in the 21st century. Moneyed interests: do not invest in Providence. Invest in children's education. Or, if you want to make money in the short term (then die ironically), invest in robots that kill dissenters, weaponizable hallucinogens, and/or "information technology."

- Now we're just being bitter and confused, but major fingers (middles all) to Landlord Shithawk, who is renovating the Winking Fox building (Rt 95, Broadway exit) and painted over the Winking Fox!!!!!!! What the hell is wrong with you? "Yes", and "I Know", that people who pay for a renovated loft space dislike that level of history and local color, but 1) it's easier for a camel to get through the eye of a needle than for a rich person to enter heaven; and 2) the Fox is one of global folklore's most classic fuckeroos, and a winking fox even moreso. This paper predicts failure for your enterprise (sorry!).

UPDATE! Juuuuuuust before this issue went to press we spotted another Wu Tang symbol, same size same color and just down the street a little bit, but this was a full W and in the center I'm pretty sure it says "TINA'S". Not sure exactly what TINA'S WU TANG is, but God bless! Bless the God the Earth the Sun and bomb the rest!

Taking the Plunge: North Dakota to Rhode Island
Heather Jackson

Having been a Great Plains resident my entire life, I made my way to Providence, Rhode Island the end of December 2014. I was officially a resident on January 1, 2015. I was born in Dickinson, a city in Western North Dakota, now populated to the point of major environmental impact and plagued by the oil drilling of the Bakken. The geography and landscape have changed in western North Dakota. Much of the great plains seem to be gone, destroyed by the oil drilling, the unexpected surge of population, and the oil companies' monopolies on the land. The land belongs to them now, not North Dakota.

I spent most of my years as a child, teenager, and young 20-something between Minot and Grand Forks (both in ND). We moved a lot because of my step-dad's restaurant work. I lived in Fargo for a few months when my mom divorced my dad. I gave birth to my daughter, as a teen, in Minot. When I was 21, I moved to Minneapolis for a few years to get my Associate degree and get out of North Dakota (it was always that: leaving North Dakota), but I found myself struggling financially to make ends up meet as a young, single mom of a toddler. Back to Grand Forks, ND I made it. I refocused my goals, graduated with my BA, and went onto graduate school and received an MA in Counseling and an MPH.

A goal of mine was to leave North Dakota. Why? It's a boring place with nothing much going on. It's conservative and I found myself feeling desperate. The things I wanted to do in life did not seem possible there. I wanted to live, not just survive. It seemed more suited for people who had decided to settle, get married, find a cushy career, and have children. If that's what a person is into, that's fine. But I'm not. I had a decent job, but it was barely enough to pay the bills. I wanted more for my life. Further, I was a former teen and single mom and I wanted to raise my daughter in a more accepting place. I was sick of the racism, homophobia, and sexism. I was sick of the judgments related to my single parent status and the constant questions: "Where is her dad?" Of course, that exists everywhere, unfortunately. But North Dakota has been known as the Mississippi of the North. I would prefer to have my daughter live out the rest of her teen years in a healthier, more diverse place.

While I had great friends in North Dakota, I needed out. Minot had/has an amazing punk scene; this is how I survived my teen years in Minot. I made great friends in Grand Forks who were involved with radical politics (including Students for a Democratic Society and Occupy). However, many of those people had already left (many made their way to New York City). Again, it came back to the fact that I wanted to raise my daughter in an accepting, diverse, and different environment. She is almost 14. I also wanted to be somewhere else for my own sanity and health.

I had money saved from a great housing assistance program. After encouragement and job post emails from a dear person in Providence, I applied for jobs on the East Coast. I applied for jobs in random cities in Connecticut, Boston, New York City, and Providence. I was doing several phone and Skype interviews. I was actually deciding to move.

Missing Providence

After doing research, Providence seemed the place for me. It was more affordable than most places I was looking at. I found an apartment using FaceTime. I spoke with someone about the best middle school for my daughter. I spent the last month in North Dakota making plans with friends and seeing them before I left. My daughter and I got rid of a lot of things before we moved. Then we packed up two U-Haul containers and shipped them to our new life in Providence. We packed my 2003 Honda Civic full of kitchen and bathroom necessities, clothes, and our 3 rabbits. We left on December 28, 2014.

We stayed the night in Fargo with my brother and early the next morning, we began our trip. We stopped in Minneapolis for lunch with one of my best friends from high school. He was also making a big move, but not for another seven months (back to Phoenix to finish graduate school). After lunch, we drove to Chicago. We got a hotel and spent the night. After a terrifying lake storm along the lakes of the Canadian border and New York state, we made it to Albany, NY and stayed the night. This was our first major road trip together. I got pregnant in high school, worked really hard, was poor and on every state assistant program I could be on, and now we were driving 26 hours to have a better life.

As we were getting closer to Providence, I was feeling better about this choice. We arrived in Providence on the evening of January 1, 2015. We picked up the keys at the apartment management office. In some ways, it felt sudden and my daughter was switching schools mid-year, but with the money I had, the encouragement I got, and the job offers: it seemed like the best choice. It was our time to get out of North Dakota.

While the skyline of Providence is small, it is pretty. Providence has the sense of a small city, with a lot to do, a lot of great communities, diversity, and active people doing awesome things. The street art is quaint. The restaurant selection is key. The fact that Providence is only a few hours from New York City is great, yet on the other hand, I can drive a different direction and end up at Lake George for camping in the woods. It's near the ocean and has beautiful beaches. It's fairly affordable. There are options for all kinds of things! There are bike riders (I bike) that fill the streets and the cars are actually polite! There are so many shows! I have seen so many amazing musicians and bands since moving here, while not all have been in Providence, most have been within a decent driving distance. When we first got here, there was no snow, and then the snow came in full force. However, I am used to it; I'm from North Dakota! The summers are not nearly as humid as they are in North Dakota. There's also a lot of history to Providence and plenty of exploring to do.

It's funny to hear about people complaining about the random things in Providence that peeve them. Of course, they can complain, but I always think to myself, "Live in North Dakota!" Providence is so much better and there's so much more going on! Yet, I can find out I know random people through other random people and am met with the comment, "That's so Rhode Island." I even know people from North Dakota who have moved to Rhode Island. Some radical artists and zinesters that I discovered while still in North Dakota live in Providence. Take my word for it, Rhode Island offers a great deal more than North Dakota.

My daughter and I live in a poorer section of the Mount Hope Neighborhood. I've heard the "watch out for Camp Street" conversations, but honestly, I haven't felt less safe than I would anywhere else. People make awful assumptions about things and I don't think living in fear of everything is a way to live life. I also don't want my daughter to have fear every time she goes outside. I chose our apartment because it was close to her middle school and I wanted her to be able to walk there and be accepted as a student there since we lived close. I plan on moving to a different neighborhood, as she wants to go to Classical High School next year. We want to live closer to that high school.

Mount Hope Neighborhood has its ups and downs. Hope Street is fun to explore on walks and has a few nice restaurants and good bars. I'm close to Brown University, which is annoying, but my daughter has access to nice walks with friends and coffee shops she can hang out at. However, I am just grateful and glad to be out of North Dakota. I will take the annoyances of the neighborhood and Brown any day.

Life can be great when you start to live it, and while I know there are limitations to this idea because of a person's situation, I feel it's true. I felt that I could start living my life in a way I wanted to when I moved here. Having met a lot of great people and making sure I get involved in local organizations to do things such as writing, guitar classes, vocal lessons, and so much more, I think taking advantage of what the city has to offer is really important. There are scholarship options available through some organizations, as well. Further, being active in the city provides the opportunity to meet new people and become involved in creating new things. Providence has been a city that has facilitated my sense of adventure, meeting new people, and living my life that way I want to.

The Order
Karen Haskell

Six wonton soups, four beef teriyakis, two shrimp fried rice, one pork fried rice, one chicken lo mein, two chop suey-chow mein mixes, one crab rangoon, one moo goo gai pan, two orders of egg rolls, one four happiness, one combination plate #20.

The total is just over $100 for 12 of us. We divide up the check. Leftovers are packed into white take-out boxes with red pagodas on each side and a single wire handle at the top.

During recent months, my mother brings a cooler and a Tupperware bowl. She transfers the take out order of chop suey-chow mein mix out of the white and red to-go boxes into the beige bowl and secures the cover. The mix will leak during the hour long ride to Connecticut if it's not in a sturdier container. She does this every other week now. It is one of my grandmother's favorite meals.

When I was small, the Hong Kong restaurant was in the somewhat seedy section of town. Buildings were sagging, Newberry's – Rhode Island's version of Woolworth's - had recently closed, and the bus stop was crowded all day long. My grandfather had grown up in the area. His childhood home was just blocks from the Hong Kong and his first job was at the Palace Theater a few doors down. He often attended mass at one of the two Catholic churches that sat directly across from each other on Main Street. Then Arctic, as the area of West Warwick is called, was lively. A beautiful theater, a busy lunch counter at Newberry's, the churches filled to capacity. To impress my grandmother, on one of their first few dates, he brought her here to the Hong Kong. And they've never stopped going.

Even with kids and a move to a different state, an hour away, my grandparents still managed to make fairly regular trips to the Hong Kong.

My dad, on date number two, asked my mom if she liked Chinese food. When her response was positive, he said: great, I know this really good place. My mom had a good laugh when he drove her to the Hong Kong.

Newly married, my parents bought a house about five miles from the Hong Kong just over the town line in Cranston. It made for easy Friday night take-out, or a Saturday dinner actually inside the restaurant which was no easy feat with three kids. It also became our Christmas Eve tradition. When I was young, before my mom returned to work full-time, she would cook, or rather attempt to cook, a big Christmas Eve dinner for us and her parents. At that time, in the late 1980s, my grandparents decided that in order to see all of their six kids and grand kids for the holiday, they needed to split up the visits over two days. My mom was granted Christmas Eve. But once she returned to work, cooking a big dinner was no longer practical. One year she suggested the Hong Kong as an alternative -- and we've never stopped going.

Every Christmas Eve we have the same waitress who knows us and our order by heart. She laughs hesitantly at my father's poorly timed jokes, and nods with him as he once again tries to remember exactly how many years we've been coming to the Hong Kong for Christmas Eve. He always throws the question to my mother: "Sue, how long have we been coming here?" And she starts in about her work schedule, and a big dinner and how we all love the food here. Then my father interrupts with: "Yeah, and this way you don't have to clean up!" He mostly means it as a joke, because he always gets a laugh from it, but he's partly right. There is a standing family joke about how as a teenager my mother would hide in the bathroom during the after dinner clean-up. The lasting retort from my fourteen-year-old mother was that her hands were too small to help.

I introduced my husband to the Hong Kong on date number three. He grumbled about the General Tso's Chicken but found an equal substitute in combination plate #20. I took him there because the food is good and cheap, and because by then downtown Arctic was starting to come alive again. New stores had moved in, Newberry's had become a clean, community-centered walk-in clinic, the two congregations consolidated and a park was planned for where the second church once stood.

I didn't know at the time that both my parents and grandparents, married 35 years and 61 years respectively, had been to the Hong Kong during the early stages of their romances. There is nothing particularly romantic about the Hong Kong Restaurant. And depending on what decade you visit the restaurant in, the surrounding downtown isn't particularly romantic either. But by date three there was clearly something in the air between my future husband and me. It's quite possible that unconsciously the Hong Kong dinner was a test. Could I picture him here on Christmas Eve? Would he happily forge a smile at my dad's recycled jokes? Could he bear the constant repetitive conversation?

Clearly he could. And now ten years later we bring our daughters here. To the same smiling waitress who remarks how big they've grown every time, even if we come in two weeks in a row.

The last few years my mother has had to call to reserve one of the big tables for Christmas Eve. There are two. One in the old part and one in the new part. The new addition was built over the 2009 Christmas holiday; the entire restaurant shut down for a week. When my mother discovered that the Hong Kong would be closed on Christmas Eve, I must admit, there was a bit of a panic. The house my parents live in is not big enough for ten or more people. We could fit ten at my house except I didn't have a table big enough. But both options required my mother and me to cook. While I didn't mind cooking, my mother was ardently looking for other alternatives. My husband, ever the hero, suggested a Chinese restaurant that he used to frequent prior to dating me. The runner-up Chinese restaurant was clean and the food decent. But it did not pass anyone's test. There was no chop suey-chow mein and the fried rice was just not right. We gladly returned to the Hong Kong the following Christmas Eve.

When calling for Christmas Eve reservations, my mom always asks for the old side. The side with the faded red leather booths, and gold-hued Asian scenes lining the walls. The double sided kitchen doors in the back. The floor clean, but scuffed. The new side is fine. The tables are a nice dark wood, sconces on the walls, a bar, and beautiful calligraphy pieces hang near each table. The lighting is dim and peaceful. We'll sit on the new side if necessary but the old side feels like home. Even my husband, who only had a few visits under his belt prior to the addition of the new side, prefers the old side. It feels lived in. In the way that a house is slightly messy: a few dishes in the sink, dust along the picture frames, a bucket of blocks left in the corner of the living room, some toothpaste stuck to the sink, a basket of a laundry yet to be done.

My grandparents first date was in 1952. They met on a double date both agreeing to go in order to help out their friends, who were very interested in one another. My grandfather likes to joke that he picked my grandmother up off the bar room floor. But the truth is, the foursome went to Rocky Point Park and danced the night away. Now a beautiful public park along the water, Rocky Point used to be an amusement park with a great dance hall, called the Palladium, and the Shoreline Dining Hall which served customers clam cakes, chowder and watermelon family-style. When I was young, my grandparents would take the entire family there (which numbered around 30 at the time) and that loud, cavernous dining hall was the only place we were all able to sit and eat at one table.

I often wonder what the inside of the Hong Kong looked like when my grandfather took my grandmother that first time. Was it lived in, the way it is now? I like to think that it has always been homey. The Hong Kong is family-run. I imagine that the Hong Kong restaurant is an immigrant success story. The hard-working, family-providing, making a new life for yourself kind. For the vast majority of my adult years, an Asian man who looks to be in his fifties has been in charge. He usually stands at the bar on the new side answering the phone, dispensing take-out orders and controlling the remote for the TV above the bar. He and some of the waitresses have accents. They often call out orders in Chinese and the younger employees chide each other in a way that only family can. I don't know for sure if the employees are family. But after all these years, they certainly feel like it.

When I was young, my family fit in one of the booths. But my family has grown which is why we need one of the big tables. The list includes: my parents, grandparents, my sister and her fiancé, my brother, his girlfriend, usually a wayward uncle or friend with no place else to go, and my husband, myself and our two pre-school age daughters. We are loud. The girls run from one lap to the next stealing French fries (yes they come with the chop suey-chow mein!) and bites of beef teriyaki, their favorite.

On Christmas Eve my grandparents drive down early in order to go to mass, often across the street from the Hong Kong at the one remaining church. The downtown has changed again. The storefronts have been redone in that posh, quaint, New England downtown sort of way. A real estate office, a kickboxing studio and a hair dresser inhabit the storefronts next to the bank with its giant Greek-like columns. A Brooks Pharmacy and CVS have steady business and a new chicken wings restaurant has been drawing crowds (with waiting lines!) to the area. Sometimes it's even hard to find parking.

This past Christmas, we offered to get take out. Drive it to Connecticut. My grandmother had been fighting cancer for three years at this point. At age 82, she remarks: what a way to go. And as usual, she is right. My grandmother is someone you would expect to live until 110. She is one of those elderly women who would swing her purse, hard, at the would-be thief, and then kick him in the shins once he was down. She can simultaneously smack my uncle in the head and hug him fiercely. She is known for her "understandings" after which no child ever repeats the offending behavior. And she once saved for five years to pay for a Disney World trip for the entire family. But by this past Christmas a mastectomy, radiation, chemotherapy, cancer drugs, had all pulled at her, bit by bit.

But she insisted on coming. To say that my grandmother loves the chop suey-chow mein from the Hong Kong restaurant would be an understatement. Every year she and my grandfather order the same thing. Two chop suey-chow mein mixes with a side of French fries and beets. Yes, red beets. My husband still doesn't understand why a Chinese restaurant serves fries and beets. This last Christmas, my grandmother ate two helpings and took leftovers home in the customary red and white take out container. She told us, as long as she could get there, she wasn't going to miss it. The food was too good, and well, the company was alright.

And that is how my grandmother is. Even now when you leave her nursing home, she will tell you to take life easy. As if the cancer cells multiplying daily in her body are commonplace. Maybe they are too common. Her youngest child, my uncle John, died of cancer at age 33. His death rocked my family. My grandfather's steadfast Catholicism shook and began to crumble. But my grandmother rebuilt it. When John's widow remarried, her new husband and subsequent daughters became my grandmother's son-in-law and her grandchildren. They are family.

My grandparents had six kids, twenty grandkids and eleven great grandkids. Attendance at Thanksgiving is mandatory. It's held in my Uncle's garage with space heaters, banquet tables, folding chairs, paper plates and plastic utensils - because who wants to wash dishes for 50+ people?

Of course no one wants to wash dishes, but every last one of us helps to set up and clean up. There is no sitting while someone else does the work unless of course you are legitimately impaired like the one and only time my mother played basketball and broke her foot. My aunts and uncles still tease her that it was yet another convenient excuse – like hiding in the bathroom.

Missing Providence

The thing is, there is no escaping my family. You can be the shy, bookish one like me and they will still find out about and show up at every poetry reading you do, or distribute multiple copies of the story that won me first prize in sixth grade. You can be like my aunt, divorced and struggling as basically a single parent to five boys and they will be there to fix your front door when it breaks, sit in the courtroom with you when the divorce is finalized; and my dad, he still takes those boys fishing. They will bail you out of trouble and get you into plenty of trouble. They will yell the loudest at your baseball game, your graduation, or just at you from across the street.

Now with my own daughters, I try to teach them about family, how they come in different shapes and sizes. That some families work together like the one owning and operating the Hong Kong Restaurant. That some are small, like my father's side. And that some have a driving force, around which the other members of the family circulate sometimes in awe, sometimes in fear, but always in love.

No one says it, but this past Christmas was my grandmother's last at the Hong Kong. The doctors say it could be weeks or months now; there is no telling. My grandmother is a fighter. But I think they are wrong. My grandmother is a lover. She loves her food, her faith, her family.

Since Christmas the cancer has spread and there are no treatment options left. My grandmother relishes food now. On Tuesday my cousin made her filet mignon for dinner. Last week my uncle brought her the lobster salad sandwich she was craving. And more often than not, my grandmother demands that my mother bring her chop suey-chow mein from the Hong Kong when she next visits.

From the Armory District to the Suburbs
Liz Kenyon

Ann McCarthy, the youngest of five children born to Gertrude and George McCarthy, grew up in a poor neighborhood in the West End of Providence. Known as the "Armory District" because of the nearby Cranston Street Armory, her neighborhood of double- and triple-decker houses was largely populated by Irish and French Canadian immigrants and by blacks.

Ann and her siblings—Regina, Frederick, Charles, and George—made the most of their Depression-era childhood, in spite of their poverty and their father's drunken behavior and abusiveness. Fred often led them in "quick math" by quickly spouting off math operations to see who could keep up. They also found refuge in the large hill on which they lived. In the cold Northeast winters, they sled on this hill, while in the spring and fall they roller skated down it. Throughout the year, Ann defiantly climbed this hill to reach her schools—Asa Messer Elementary, Gilbert Stuart Middle School, and finally the prestigious Classical High School, which required passing an entrance exam and teacher references.

Asa Messer was Ann's favorite school, for it was here that she learned her life-long love of reading. The school, a three-story Queen Anne brick edifice, was designed by architects William R. Walker & Son, who were also responsible for most of the Rhode Island public buildings from that period, including the nearby Cranston Street Armory.

Asa Messer prepared Ann well for the rigorous academic requirements of Classical High School where she admirably completed the requisite four years of Latin, English, and French. She also handsomely managed her studies of the classics, albeit she struggled with calculus and physics.

During her free time, Ann practiced both the piano and her Catholic faith. For example, during the Lenten season, she joined her sister Regina (Jean) in walking several miles to visit seven local Catholic churches every Holy Thursday. At each of their visits, including their visit to the Cathedral of St. Peter and Paul on Fenner Street, they humbly said their rosary. Of course, as "good Catholics", they also attended weekly penance at their local church, St. Charles, on the corner of Dexter Street.

As a joyful Saturday excursion, Ann would take the trolley car to downtown Providence, where she secretly met her boyfriend George at the Outlet Department Store clock. George would treat her to a movie at one of the theatres, such as the Modern Theatre, and then they would share a soda fountain beverage.

Sadly, like many of her neighbors, Ann could not afford college. And so she and George ended their relationship when he went away to college. But she soon met and married a new love, Joseph Kenyon. Joseph was a stationary engineer nine years her senior who had recently served in the U.S. Navy in World War II. About the same time, Jean married James Unsworth, also a Navy man, who had served in the Normandy invasion.

With the improved economy of the early 1950's, city dwellers were moving to the suburbs, where home ownership was now possible for many. The two sisters and their new spouses joined the migration and built small Cape Cod houses next door to each other amongst the farmlands of Warwick. But while Ann escaped the city, she did not escape the abuse that she had long suffered at the hands of her father.

George McCarthy was an alcoholic who regularly abused his wife and children. Initially, the abuse was mild. But after one fateful night, it became brutal.

On a cold winter's night during prohibition, George invited friends over to their home for "bathtub gin."

George, while poor, was very intelligent and well-educated. As the first-born son of an affluent Irish family, he followed tradition and attended seminary school in Ireland. But when he returned to the States, rather than enter the priesthood, he married Gertrude, who was an orphan. His parents, furious with his decisions, disowned him. George told them to go to hell and cast off his high-society lifestyle for a much simpler life.

A great conversationalist who always carried a slide rule and an Esperanto dictionary in his pockets, George was endeared to men of all walks of life. Consequently, his guests that fateful night included a doctor and other professionals. Thus when his wife, Gertrude, pleaded with him to get a doctor for George Jr., he turned to the doctor who was present. The drunken doctor examined George Jr., and declared him fine. Poor George Jr., age 8, had pneumonia and died during the night.

Subsequently, George went from being primarily a "happy drunk" to a terribly abusive father and husband. His wife Gertrude, son Frederick, and daughter Jean suffered the worst of his physical abuse. But Ann and Charlie were no strangers to his actions. Nor was their dog.

For Ann, the abuse continued with her new husband, Joseph. One night, Joseph was drunk on whiskey and threatened her with a gun. Terrified, Ann took their infant son Frederick and left Joseph. She did not return until he promised never to drink hard liquor again. Joseph kept his promise until his death some fifty years later. During those fifty years, Joseph never laid a hand on Ann; however, he was very verbally abusive to her. And so while Ann rose above the poverty of the Armory District to a middle-class life in the suburbs, she never fully broke free from the abuse of her childhood.

New Armory [17]

Dear Urban Chicken Farmer of Providence
Amanda Faith Poirier

Dear Urban Chicken Farmer of Providence,

The Order of the Coop is writing to you to request rooster visitations. We have no objection to our life in your backyard coop, including our duties to lay eggs and eat pests. We want to continue to do our job.

However, we cannot lay our eggs and lay them well without a little stimulation. We are either wound up too tight or not wound up at all. We are a mess. We pace inside the coop and around it. Some days we wander into the street, our beaks pecking against the concrete. We do not know we are in the street until a person screams or a car horn beeps and tires swerve. Yesterday, Sister Gertrude reported Sister Prudence had been struck and flattened by a car. She was a great hen. Laid wholesome eggs.

We do not blame you. We should have seen it coming. A week ago, a tandem bicycle hit Sister Chastity. She sustained minor injuries, so we shrugged it off.

We cannot ignore the signs any longer. We hens have been starved of male feathers for too many years. We need rooster visitations and we need them now!

Look, we understand, roosters cannot live with us. Trust us, the arrangement is acceptable, perfect actually. We do not want roosters coming into our hen house, flapping their wings around like they own the place. We also do not wish to wake up to their brash, inconsiderate *cock-a-doodle-doo* every single morning. It is so typical rooster—demanding everyone to look at him. We hens require our beauty sleep because some chickens actually work around the coop. We require time to reflect, for without that our eggs will not be whole. That does not mean we wish to be alone all the time.

Based on our read of the Chicken Ordinance, which amends Chapter 4 of the Ordinances entitled Animals and Fowl Section 1, there is no preclusion of rooster visitations. We are not asking for a lengthy visit. One-hour tops, if his strut is strong. We swear we will continue to meet our quota of five eggs per week. In fact, we expect we will lay more eggs—healthier too, the more roosters we see. As we see it, it is advantageous to both sides. The more eggs we produce, the more ways for you to enjoy them.

Supply us a macho Spanish rooster and we will lay spicy eggs for a Huevos Rancheros breakfast feast.

Bring us a Japanese warrior rooster and we will lay large eggs for a Tamagoyaki fit for a samurai.

Get us a German firm rooster and we will lay sweet eggs for a Quiche Lorraine dinner your neighbors will smell and long for with envy.

Send us an Indian dancing rooster and we will lay sour eggs for a Guddu Pulusu that will leave your mouth watering for more.

Deliver us the Rhode Island Red—the prince of roosters—and we will lay eggs of any style or size. Not that size matters. If the rooster can waltz, then he can rock our coop anytime.

We request one rooster per sister hen. We chickens refuse to share cock. No, we are not selfish. We share our feed and coop with grace. We range together and never fight. The Order is a collective of smart and forward-thinking sisters. If we are forced to share a rooster, the life in and outside of the coop will get ugly fast.

Please deliver us one *cock-a-doodle-doo* per week—it is all we need and frankly all we can stand—for each sister hen. If you fulfill our request, then we promise to make you the proud owner of the best hens who produce the most mouthwatering eggs in all of Providence.

    Sincerely,
    The Order of the Coop

Missing Providence

Acknowledgments
Thomas Brendler

To Fifth Street, to every house on Fifth Street
Two-families and triple deckers, the one with the garage
Maybe an old barn, the old spruce pruned as high as a stepladder, weeping white sap
To the rabbits blinking, then gone up the sideyards

To the hum of the hospital, the cancer ward's rooftop HVAC
To the ambulance lights sweeping, languid, sirens silenced within radius
Chains looped from chassis to ground their machines, like ringed knuckles

To the loading dock, the yew hedges, every panel of siding
To Silence-of-the-Lambs Guy shining his candyshell Mustang, sputtered up the block, elbow loose and thrumming,
Around and back

To the lavender holding on at the curb, the parking cops, the fringe tree
Our daughter's umbilicus entwined in its roots for good luck

To the Sorkins, she ululating for her cat in the near-darkness, in Russian, over the fence, into the hidden crowns
He continuing to say he'll complete the downspout on my side of his garage and continuing to never get to it
To the light behind their backboard, casting eclipse down their driveway like the ghost of some skull
To the scrape and crack of their son's skateboard in the hot twilight jolting the baby as she nursed

To our daughter's bedroom empty except for picture hooks and the mop we came back for the day after we moved

To the fake cobwebs snagged to the birch trunk
The clawtracks of the squirrels along the rail of the fence

To Mr. Halper striding along the parking lot to Mishkon Tfiloh in his big hat and boots
Past the healing garden, past the patients smoking in their billowing johnnies
At dusk

To his son in his attic room above our yard feeling his way through the *Sweet Child of My-yi-yine* intro over and over and over
As we weeded, shouldering the stroller toward deeper shade

To Anna out pacing, cursing, then gunning her rusty Volvo, taking the turns wide,
    not missing a draw
To the Bell Biv Devoe LP washed up in our pachysandra
To the sunburst cracks from the draping limb the knot now almost closed
A boom for a slick, or maybe a lariat

To the cloud of feathers in the backyard
Almost a shadow on the silvery bristles
On a low branch the shape of an owl

MOURNING GLORY
Adele Bourne

She drew children to her as she listened to herself.
Indifferent to appearances, she did what she pleased,

wrote songs in Portuguese she had picked up on the playground,
performed on the gamelan, the clavier, the drums.

Teens talked to her of problems with their great pulsations.
Young men loved her as she loved each in turn.

She gave up medication for trance and meditation,
emptied her cupboards for the hungry on the streets.

She thought her cat a vegetarian, and that anyone could live
on water, grass, and air, with proper breath control.

Perceptions so acute, she lived seven lives at once.
The only limits she'd accept — sunrise and sunset.

She took the bullet train, speeding toward the West.
Those left behind — Ah well, they could take the bus.

Peculiar Reflection
Jennifer L. Geller

"There is probably no Scottish county so underrated as Clackmannan," wrote John Carvel in 1944. "One would never gather," he continued, that "the slopes rising from the plain of Clackmannan were grander than those in any other part of the range…hillscape, romantic river stretches, deep ravines, woodlands, fertile carselands, all are here." Yet their pastoral sublime-cloaked coal pits, textile mills, whisky distilleries, iron works, silver mines. These hills, the Ochils, now towering over disintegrating post-industrial villages, the River Devon straggling along their edges all seemed irrationally familiar to me, but the landscape remained elusive.

In the *Old Statistical Account*, I read of the "fituation and fingular construction of the Devon iron works, begun in July 1792. A fteep bank rifes more than 50 feet above the level of the river. The feveral parts of the works have been formed in this bank, by excavations made in the rock." I come across an 1861 account by a life-long resident of the county, who describes "a most salubrious locality where rocky glens and cascades abut on the factories." Would that I could be Carvel, "looking back across the valley from the main road into Tillicoultry, pick[ing] out the old slag-heap of the Iron Works projecting toward the river." Instead I must rely on an undated photo taken from the tip itself, superimposing the magisterial ruins of the works onto the Ochils beyond, or slog over the remnants of the bing, ruins no longer holding court, pounding cores for soil samples in the pouring rain, seeking the summit of Ben Cleuch through the mist when I pause to catch my breath. Beneath my wellies the woody grass roots itself in soft river soil, blanketing bits of brick and crumbling coal, smothering still deeper faint voices of arsenic and lead, suppressing the story of this land. Above/below, visible/invisible—the paradoxes will not resolve themselves. These are edgelands, peculiar and enigmatic, a reflection of me. Resolution will rob us of our identity.

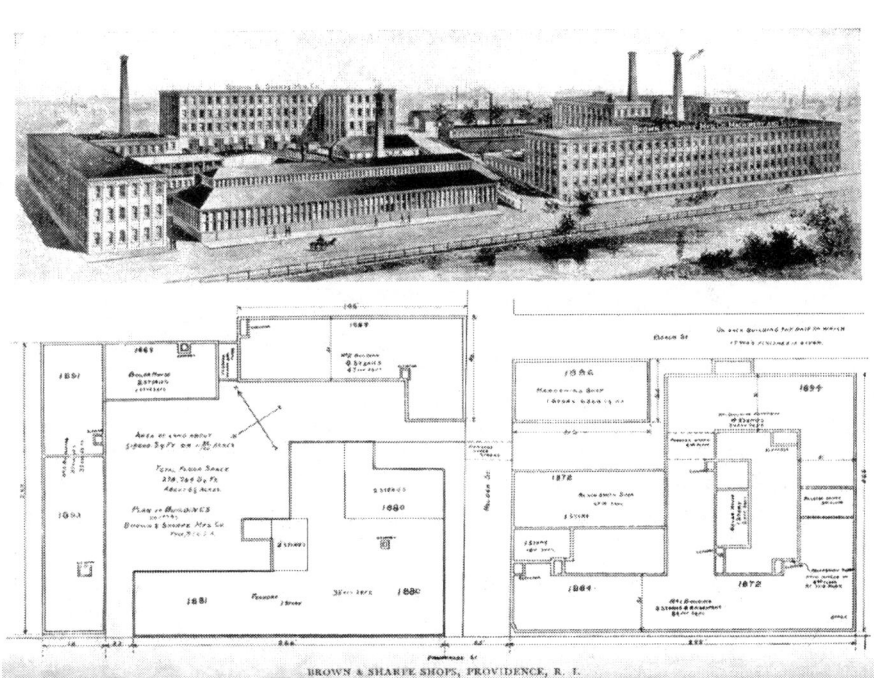
Browns & Sharpe Shops, 1896 [18]

We Move the Machines
For the Robinson Men
by Claire Robinson

Inside the mill, circa 1872, full of worn-out, dust
-infested machines where women worked among stale air
making elastic thread—we are here, figuring out the scene.
It is all about rigging, methodical execution
to avoid something crashing down, someone crushed, or losing a limb
the way some mill women did to the machines. A man
in an expensive car waits for us to shepherd these looms
into containers bound for factories in India or Peru—
the world still wants affordable thread, no matter
where it is shipped from, it will arrive as always.

Almost everything here is an antique: the beams, the gantry,
creaking floors complaining in the manner of old men.
No matter, they still fulfill their duties, the way thin blood
continues its travels around an ailing body
or geese return to the city's edge to peck at asphalt
where a sedgy pond once was. Just do their job, the way we do, lifting
these ancient monsters onto beams and dollies
and pushing them across space to the gantry. In the air
they almost look graceful and good, giant steel sparrows
caught in straps, more than useful looms.
Their greasy metal sides are cut across by shafts of light,
and shine. They are transformed, suspended and stripped
of everything except how they hang here, oversized
technological ornaments, weightlessly stunning.

I think I understand what it is to be shaped by unknown forces
for some narrow reason, to work for ages, sometimes maiming those
you were meant to help, until one moment you are launched out,
your eyes full of dazzle, above that world which enclosed you—
and your breath catches in your throat but still you know
sometime soon you will be set down again, to get back
to the small thing you do so well, without tiring, without complaint.

Frequency Writers

Missing Providence

REFERENCES

1. Cover by Ben Williams
2. "Industrial Trust Company under construction, Providence, RI", VM013_WC0264-1, Rhode Island Photograph Collection, Providence Public Library, Providence, RI.
3. "Interstate 195 under construction", VM013.GF3128, Rhode Island Photograph Collection, Providence Public Library, Providence, RI.
4. "Greetings from Providence, Rhode Island", PC9130-13, Rhode Island Postcard Collection, Providence Public Library, Providence, RI.
5. "Sheraton Biltmore Hotel in hurricane", VM013.GC2142, Rhode Island Photograph Collection, Providence Public Library, Providence, RI.
6. Photograph by Nada Samih-Rotondo
7. "Old Hoyle Tavern formerly at the junction of Westminster and Cranston Sts., Providence, R.I. ", PC7147, Rhode Island Postcard Collection, Providence Public Library, Providence, RI.
8. Photo of work by Alexander Smith
9. "Brown & Sharpe Mfg. Co. Providence, R.I. ", PC6791, Rhode Island Postcard Collection, Providence Public Library, Providence, RI.
10. "Providence River and harbor by night, Providence, R.I. ", PC7076, Rhode Island Postcard Collection, Providence Public Library, Providence, RI.
11. "Holy Rosary Church, Providence, R.I. ", PC6889, Rhode Island Postcard Collection, Providence Public Library, Providence, RI.
12. All images in TRI-X Providence by Susan Tacent
13. "Capitol, Providence, R.I. ", PC8154, Rhode Island Postcard Collection, Providence Public Library, Providence, RI.
14. Ihlder, John. *Hassan Street*. 1916. John D. Rockefeller, Jr. Library, Brown University, Providence. *The Houses of Providence, a Study of Present Conditions and Tendencies, with Notes on the Surrounding Communities and Some Mill Villages*. Providence: Snow & Farnham, 1916. 2. Print.
15. "City Hall, Providence, R.I. ", PC6961, Rhode Island Postcard Collection, Providence Public Library, Providence, RI.
16. Ihlder, John. *Triptych*. 1916. John D. Rockefeller, Jr. Library, Brown University, Providence. *The Houses of Providence, a Study of Present Conditions and Tendencies, with Notes on the Surrounding Communities and Some Mill Villages*. Providence: Snow & Farnham, 1916. 28. Print.
17. "New Armory, Providence, R.I. ", PC6426, Rhode Island Postcard Collection Providence Public Library, Providence, RI.
18. Arnold, Horace L. *Browns & Sharpe Shops, Providence RI, 1896*. Digital image. *Wikimedia Commons*. "Modern Machine-Shop Economics." in Engineering Magazine 11. 1896, 20 Nov. 2014. Web. 14 Apr. 2015.

Made in the USA
Middletown, DE
16 October 2015